The Keto Meal Prep Manual

Make-Ahead Meals to Save You Time and Help You Stick to Your Diet

Andrea Adams

Table of Contents

Introduction

Thank you for purchasing this book, *Keto Meal Prep*. I hope that you will find it extremely useful on your journey through your Keto diet.

We all know the problem with diets – that our great intentions fade over time and with the pressures of daily life. But this book helps you to find a way past this, because it is not just a recipe book (although it provides plenty of tasty versions of these).

This book will provide detailed advice on prepping your food for a Keto diet. This means anything from sorting portion sizes or chopping up vegetables in advance, to preparing full meals to freeze or just remove from the fridge, heat and enjoy; all will be covered.

Eating is more than just a way to give the body energy. This book will show that it can still be tasty and fun, even when following a diet.

The purpose of this book is to provide you with all of the tools to make your diet work for your schedule instead of the other way around.

In this book, I've really emphasized SIMPLE recipes where you can do most of the prep ahead of time. Many recipes are designed to allow you to get on with other jobs while the food cooks.

The Keto Diet is one that builds on a number of previous ideas around the value of a low carb high fat food intake, and this focus is a well-established idea. There is a lot of evidence that the Keto diet can provide quick results in terms of weight loss, energy improvements, and healthy living in general. These meals really focus on healthy, and tasty, eating.

By reading the prepping section of the book, finding your own prepping day or days, planning meals carefully and shopping sensibly, you really will save time and money while enjoying fresh tasting, vibrant meals that will make cooking a joy and eating a thrill.

Prepping can change your life. Seriously. Having food ready to heat and eat means that you avoid that dilemma of whether to cook or get a take out. Everything is there, in the fridge, ready to go. The quickest option is to eat in, with your own freshly cooked food. This will eliminate a lot of temptations that lead you away from your dietary goals.

A Little Bit of History

The keto diet – or ketogenic diet to give it its full name – has a good deal of history behind it. It first came into play as far back as the 1920's, when the medicinal benefits were used for the treatment of epilepsy.

It was known that fasting was beneficial to this condition, but (clearly) could offer only short-term benefits. However, it was found that similar improvements in the condition came about when patients followed a ketogenic diet.

The development of anti-convulsion drugs meant that it fell out of favour just before the outset of the second World War. However, there were still benefits for children and those who did not respond to drugs.

In the early 60's, research demonstrated that there were health advantages in the way the body produces and uses fats when people ate a low carbohydrate diet.

Nowadays, we know that followers of the Ketogenic diet will not only lose weight, because they use their fats more effectively, but will gain many of the other advantages of this healthy eating pattern (including better skin, better digestion and improved levels of energy).

So go ahead, read and make use of this book – it could be a turning point in your diet and eating habits. Unlike many other diets, eating in a Keto-friendly way is completely safe provided you eat a good balance of healthy foods, fats, and consume at least a base-level of carbs .

Let's get started on the first day of the new you!

Getting Ready – Meal Prepping

Introduction:

Meal prepping is perhaps the best way of ensuring that you stick to your diet. Let's be honest, we all live busy lives and returning from work knowing you need to start from scratch for that evening's meal is wearing.

Food prepping will save you time and help you to stick to your diet.

In the end, most of us will opt to eat out, get take-out or find the old candy bar hidden in the cupboard, and the left-over pizza from the weekend.

But if your meal has already been prepped, it becomes the default option to eat, because it is the easiest. Thin about that! Suddenly eating a healthy and delicious meal you've already prepared is easier than ordering take-out. How awesome is that?!

By food prepping, we mean anything that can help you to save time when it comes to getting your dinner ready to eat. At one extreme, it means having the meal ready, so it just needs to be reheated, or if it is a salad, simply tossed and dressed. At the other, even measuring out portions of walnuts, or chopping an onion ready for cooking, is prep. The more you can do, the more time you will save in the long run.

There are procedures you can learn which will help with your meal prepping. We will run through these, including advice on how to make prepping as simple, time effective and enjoyable as possible.

We will also offer prepping advice in the nearly 60 recipes that follow, which will offer everything from breakfast, through lunch and on to dinner, freezer food and throw together last-minute meals.

1) Choose Your Prepping Day In Advance

This then becomes a part of your routine. We all have different regimens and commitments, but a Sunday can be a good day. Most people are not at work, and an hour or two can generally be found easily.

Make it fun: Find a good podcast, or put on your favourite music, and it can be great fun. You have the motivation of knowing that you are preparing food which will help you to achieve your end goals, be it weight loss, extra energy or just a better general fitness.

Teamwork makes the dream work: If a couple of you are on the diet in your household, working together can make it even more enjoyable. For instance, if you and your partner are on this dietary journey together, it can be a great bonding experience to prep together. Pump up your favourite tunes, start chopping veggies, and portioning things out—not only are you ensuring you will stick to your diet that week, but you're spending quality time with your loved one and working together towards a common goal.

It will depend on your meal options, but it is possible that your dinners and lunches might not last until the end of the week. There are two ways of dealing with this. You could have a second, smaller prep time, perhaps on an evening where you know you will be in, or when it is usually a quiet day of work.

Another way is to plan your meals so that the longest lasting food is eaten at the end of the week. Later, we will give a detailed breakdown of how long various foods will survive in the fridge, both cooked and raw and offer advice on freezing as well. We will also give an indication of how long a meal will keep once prepared and, where appropriate, cooked. This information will be of great help as you plan your keto diet menu.

Choosing your prepping day can help you to establish a good routine. Just like with working out, the more you can set in place a plan, the less likely you'll be to deviate from it or fail to execute.

2) Plan Ahead

Good planning helps you to save time and money.

The Keto diet for rapid weight loss, is not recommended to be sustained long term. Your body is not designed to be in a permanent state of ketosis. It's better for intermittent cleanses. However, there are many aspects of the keto diet that can be implemented in daily life that are great for long term plans to maintain once you've reached your desired weight. Therefore, you could roughly draft out a two or three-week cycle of meals, repeating them as necessary.

That way, you are not wasting time (and money) buying food which will go to waste, and you will have enough in stock for your needs. There is nothing more frustrating than running out of an ingredient which is necessary for your recipes.

3) Stick With The Basics

The meals that work best with prepping are the simplest ones. Complex recipes not only keep less well, but take longer to prepare. You could reward yourself for reaching your goals by treating yourself with a fancy meal on the prep day as a way of encouraging you to keep at it. But as the week develops, go for the simpler recipes.

Of course, one of the advantages of the Keto diet is that the healthy, high fat foods often keep fairly well.

4) Be An Effective Shopper

Having a good list helps you to shop effectively

Check Dates: This is especially important for food prepping. Stores often mark down foods that are approaching expiration, but unless you're planning on eating them the same day, avoid these "sales." Keep in mind that you're not actually saving yourself ANY money if these foods just spoil in your refrigerator when you could have paid 20 cents more for fresher food. Make sure that shopping becomes a skill in which you are an expert. Buy foods with a good 'Use By' date.

Stay well-stocked: Make sure your pantry always has plenty of the ingredients you need. A good way to guage this is to be aware of ingredients you use a lot that are staples, and just always keep a supply of them on hand (for me, a few of these are: canned tomatoes, garlic, onions, frozen veggies, eggs, cheese, olive oil, butter etc.)

Stick to the list: Have a list, so that you don't forget things, and aren't tempted to buy something you shouldn't! Big supermarket stores are masters at getting their customers to do this. Go into the store aware that they're trying to get you to fill up your cart with things you don't need and don't belong in your diet. There are even smart phone apps that will help you with your grocery lists.

Routine: As with your prepping, have one or two shopping days per week. For example, you could do a "big shop" at a large supermarket one day for all your meats and non-perishables and to restock your staples, and then stop at the local farmer's market on your way home from work another day to get all your fresh produce.

Routine is everything when it comes to dieting.

5) Invest In A Cool Bag

Avoid a squashed lunch by buying a cool box or bag.

The chances are, the meals that you have prepped for lunches will be taken to work with you. Have an appropriate carrying bag, insulated of course.

One of the keys to good prepping is about making life easier. If it takes twenty minutes of packing and re-packing when you are tired in the morning, then the same when you get to work and need your laptop, then the prepping will seem counterproductive, and you could end up buying a pre-packed sandwich from the local deli.

But if you have your food bag into which you can slip your ready prepped lunch, life is much easier.

Summary

So, to summarise this section:

- Prepping saves time, and it means you are much more likely to stick to your diet.
- To make it work most efficiently, be organised and establish a routine. Outline the meals for the week, prepare a shopping list and shop accordingly. Set aside your 'prepping time' and have an easy way of transporting food where necessary.

In a way, the busier you are the more important prepping becomes. Because you can tell yourself you do not HAVE to stick to your diet, as much as you want to. It will be that part of your life that goes by the wayside if you become stretched too thin. Prepping will stop that, because using the prepared food will become the default way of working, it will be the easiest way for you to eat.

When Prepping Turns Bad: Common Issues That Can Arise with Food Prepping and How to Avoid Them

Prepping occasionally has more risks than a cut finger...but not often.

Prepping is without a doubt the best way to get your meals ready when you are on the Keto diet, or any other diet in fact. Indeed, prepping is the best way of eating well and eating healthy whatever diet you are on—heck—even if you're not dieting.

But sometimes things can go wrong. Here are some of the most common ways this can happen, and how best to overcome and avoid these problems.

It Takes Too Long And Is Therefore Not Worth The Effort

Ingredients vs. Meals: Good planning is the key here. For some people, it helps to focus on ingredients rather than meals. Rather than preparing separate meals, start by preparing separate ingredients, so chop all the carrots you need for the week, put them aside, then go on to another ingredient.

Get the worst over with: Start with the things you like doing least, so if you find weighing out nuts tedious in the extreme, do it first and get it out of the way.

The point at which you get to put all the ingredients together into recipes is then deeply satisfying. This method means that you both save time and get the worst jobs over with quickly.

Be Strategic with Storage: Pack your refrigerator efficiently, perhaps by meal or by food type, depending on how much assembly you will need to do later when you get the food ready to eat. This can save time when you are busy in an evening, or are desperate to get the cooking done. Instead you can settle down with a nice glass of wine.

Be Realistic: start with simple recipes until you get the hang of it. If youre the type of person that always underestimates how much time you need to do something, you will definitely want to take note of this. Therefore, start with simple recipes that you can easily prep, and increase in complexity and difficulty as you become more accustomed to this way of cooking and eating.

Although there is an initial time investment, food prepping saves time in the end.

Keeping Food Safe

Not even this guy will keep you safe from poorly kept food.

This is of crucial importance of course, and when you are prepping food for a long period (4-7+ days) you will be using lots of ingredients, it's something you have to be careful of. However, this type of prepping is completely safe provided you follow the guidelines below.

- Keep raw meats away from other ingredients.
- Wash your hands, utensils and your worksurfaces after handling raw meats.
- Even if they are to be stored in sealed containers, raw meats should be stored at the bottom of the fridge, so they cannot drip onto other foods.
- Check the Use By' dates on food, and stick to them (especially with meat and dairy) produce you can be a little more lenient with especially if you are cooking it as opposed to eating it raw.
- Check the table for storage later in this book, and follow it closely.

Make your own labels for the freezer and fridge to make sure you use food in time, saving waste and reducing the risk of food poisoning.

- Complete the hand, surface and utensil washing procedures with raw vegetables as well as meats. Although less common, these can also contain bacteria as well as pesticides which can be harmful.
- Wash raw vegetables and fruit before consuming.
- Keep raw foods away from 'ready to eat' foods, such as salad or nuts, since you will not be washing these before consumption.
- If you are cooking food as a part of your prep, make sure that it is thoroughly cooked to avoid contamination.
- Check re-heating guidelines for foods. Some are fine, others, such as already frozen foods, are less safe.

As you can see, this is all common sense, but can be easily forgotten when you're in a rush.

I Will Just Put It Off Until Tomorrow, I Am So Busy Today

A common and disastrous mistake. Once you have put something off once, even if you still did do it the next day, it becomes easier to do so again in the future.

Get in the habit of sticking to your prepping regime. Once you put something off, it becomes easier to do so in the future.

Remember, you will have chosen your prepping day because it works best with your schedule. It must then be a priority; so, if at all possible, put off something else rather than the food prepping.

We all know that one of the hardest aspects of a diet is consistency and you need to give yourself the very best chance of doing this.

Food Gets Soggy

Certainly, it can be true, some water-heavy foods will get soggy as the week goes on. However, by using glass storage containers rather than plastic one's food will stay crisp for longer. Also, consider how you store that food.

Salad in a jar is more than just a pretty sight.

If you are using vegetables, put the heaviest items at the bottom, and cover the top with a paper towel to soak up moisture.

Putting meat onto skewers is a great way of ensuring portion size but also popping them under the grill for a few minutes before eating takes no time and will make the food crispy and fresh tasting.

As suggested earlier, prep food which stays fresh the least amount of time for the early part of the week.

Careful planning can make your pre-prepared food as tasty as that which is freshly made, plus you get the convenience of the time you have saved, and the knowledge that you just need to pop it out of the fridge and, perhaps, give it a brief heat in the microwave, on the stove, under the grill or in the oven.

I Worry About the Dangers Of Storing Meat

That is a good thing, because it is definitely the case that there is greater risk with meat products than other products because of the bacteria (including e-coli) which it contains.

And to be worried means that you are much more likely to take the precautions that make it safe.

We have seen above the importance of washing everything, including yourself, after working with raw meat.

Stick to the points below and it will be completely safe.

- Do not wash raw meat – the water could spray around, spreading contamination.
- Do not re-freeze defrosted meat.
- Store meat separately, even cooked, if keeping for a while.
- After cooking, cool quickly and place in a sealed container in the fridge.
- When reheating, it needs at least two minutes at 70 degrees Celsius to be safe.
- If you are using defrosted meat, it must be consumed within twenty-four hours.

Follow these guidelines, and all will be well.

10 Tips For Speeding Up The Prepping Process

Anything that makes the process of prepping quicker and easier will be a must for those taking on this task. Here are some top tips for speeding up the job.

1) Prep The Meals Before You Prep Your Food

We touched briefly on this earlier in the book. Spending a bit of time planning what you will eat on each day will save a lot of time when it comes to shopping, and prepping your food. A simple table will do the job, with days of the week and the three meals (plus a snack if you are ultra-efficient.

Thus, Monday is not always fish—unless that is what you really want. Do a two or three-week cycle before moving on to repeats. This keeps your eating plan fresh and exciting, making your diet still easier to commit to.

2) Make use of the freezer

Your freezer is for more than ice cream. Cooking five portions of a meal usually doesn't take any longer than cooking one portion. So, if you are cooking a nice, tasty curry, cook up extra portions, spread them out and freeze in advance. I have an entire section of this book devoted to freezer meals, so stay tuned. We all know the pleasure that is to be gained (and why not?) from seeing a pile of perfectly positioned containers in the fridge. You can double the joy by having the same ready in the freezer.

3) Snacks Need To Be Considered

The great plan you have worked out goes down the tubes if you're constantly snacking on sugary or unhealthy snacks between meals for that extra energy boost or to hold off those hunger pangs. There are two ways of handling this:

Make your meals bigger. The great thing about the keto diet, is you can eat a lot. You can eat your fill of satisfying food and still lose weight. Plus your body responds best when you stick to a routine of eating—it knows how to conserve and expend energy, but if you eat small meals and sporadically snack, your body will be confused and your energy and hunger levels will be a problem.

If you must snack, then you have to prep keto-friendly snacks. I suggest that you first focus on tackling your meal prep before you consider snack prepping.

4) Choosing Safe Containers

We are learning more and more about the dangers of BPA. This stands for bisphenol A, and is the industrial chemical used in certain plastics. It leaks into food, especially when the container is heated. We are still finding out about the long-term impacts, but it is certainly something that should be avoided whenever possible. Opt for glass and metal storage if you can, and do not heat your food in plastic.

5) Make Your Containers Work For You

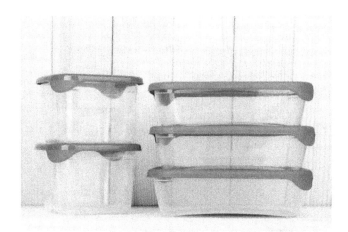

Having containers with good lids which will stack in the fridge will help you save time when prepping.

We are all about being efficient when it comes to meal prepping. What could be more annoying than the following two things? Number one, the lids don't fit properly on the containers. Number two, the containers don't fit in the fridge. To address the first, as tempting as it could be to use old ice cream pots for your food storage, not only are they likely to be alive with BPA, but very quickly the ultra-thin plastic will crack, and a tight fit will be lost. It is worth investing a small sum in better quality containers. Secondly, get out the measuring tape and work out how much space you have in the fridge, and buy containers that fit.

6) Start Small

Your first meal prepping experience will define your attitude to it. You wouldn't start training for a marathon by running twenty-six miles, but would build up to it. The same with food prepping. Start with a day or two, and as you see the benefits building up to a whole week will seem an ever more sensible route.

7) Use Frozen Vegetables

They generally have most of the same health benefits of fresh veegetables, and will save a lot of time when it comes to preparation – provided, of course, that they are pre-cut.

8) There's Nothing Smoother Than A Smoothie

Measure out the ingredients, pop them into a securable plastic bag and stick them in the freezer. They make a perfect breakfast, or even light weekend lunch. Quick, tasty, nutritional and easy, dismiss the smoothie at your peril.

9) Muffin-ization

Another easy way to portion quickly and in a form that stores easily is by using muffin tins. We will include some recipes later, but cooking up the ingredients in a muffin tin can make for perfect portions and storage.

A simple muffin tin, about $2 from a large store, can be a brilliant help when you cook in bulk.

10) *Speed Things Up With A Slow Cooker*

A slow cooker will more than repay its investment in terms of the convenience it offers.

This inexpensive kitchen tool is a brilliant way of getting food prep done more quickly. Throw in the ingredients, turn it on, leave it to cook for the best part of a day, and simply serve and eat. A seven-quart cooker is big enough to cook ten portions at a time.

On top of everything else, the resulting meal will be delicious and is especially comforting on a cold night or after a tough day at work when we all are need our comfort food fix.

Meal Planning Vs. Meal Prepping

We have discussed, a couple of times now, meal planning. Even though this book is about meal prepping, tt is worth spending a little time exploring the difference between these two important aspects of your diet.

Both are crucial, and are things we strongly recommend, to help you stick to your aims and achieve your goals. However, they are slightly different things.

Meal planning is the preparation time spent ensuring that what you eat fits your dietary aims and needs. So, it will be identifying the ingredients for recipes that deliver food that, in this situation, fit with the requirements of the keto diet. The other important part of meal planning is devising a plan or schedule of your meals—for some, that means planning out each of your three meals for the next 2-3 weeks.

Meal prepping is the next stage. Once your meals for the week have been planned and once those ingredients have been located and purchased you prep the ingredients in advance so that the meal can be ready to eat with a minimum amount of effort.

If you are trying to eat healthy with a low carb diet, it is much easier to stick to it if there is less work to do to get your meals ready in the moment. Meal prepping also means that you are much less likely to snack, get take away or eat out. These tend to be the ideas of last resort when you do not feel like cooking, or nothing appeals to you in the fridge. If your meal is already there, and just needs re heating, you are much more likely to eat it, thus sticking to your diet.

At the same time, if your meal planning is effective, all your meals will be of the correct portion size for your needs, and will contain all the right mixtures of fats, proteins, vitamins etc. to ensure that you achieve your dietary goals.

Your meal planning also eradicated the decision anxiety that comes from deciding what you will eat for any given meal, and makes food shopping less wasteful.

The purpose of this book is to provide you with recipes that can be prepped ahead. You can easily create your own meal plan from the recipes that appeal to you, or see one of my other books that includes detailed meal plans.

Ingredients And Storage Information

Here we will look at various food types and advise how they should be stored, and for how long they keep fresh.

Store raw meats on the bottom shelf of the fridge, to prevent drips onto other foodstuffs.

The information below relates to a safe storage period for meat and fish. If buying food ready packaged, use the dates on the packets.

Food	Raw In Fridge	Cooked In Fridge	Raw In Freezer	Cooked In Freezer
Beef	4 to 5 days	4 to 5 days	6 to 9 months	3 to 4 months
Pork	4 to 5 days	4 to 5 days	4 to 6 months	3 to 4 months
Chicken	2 to 3 days	3 to 5 days	3 to 4 months	8 to 9 months
Lamb	4 to 5 days	4 to 5 days	6 to 9 months	3 to 4 months
Other Poultry	2 to 3 days	2 to 3 days	3 to 4 months	3 to 4 months
Sliced Processed Meats	N A	3 to 5 days	N A	1 to 2 months
Fatty Fish (e.g. Salmon)	1 to 2 days	3 to 4 days	2 to 3 months	4 to 6 months
Lean Fish (e.g. Cod)	1 to 2 days	3 to 4 days	6 months	6 months

Fruit and veg are usable until they start to go soft and soggy. Typically, fruits will keep for up to a week un-prepped, four to five days prepped. Hard vegetables will last for a week with ease. Salad leaves will start to go soggy once prepared, if you follow the storage advice given earlier, after about three to four days.

Salad dressings, nuts and seeds will last for much longer, even when prepped. Seeds and nuts will also keep well out of the fridge for a long period.

Foods Best Not To Be Prepped

Some foods do not lend themselves to prepping. When it comes to freezing cooked eggs (as opposed to raw), salad foods, dairy or cream (unless it is whipped), mayonnaise and low-fat dairy products, know that these items will not fare well.

Freezer burn is also a risk, especially with raw chicken. This makes the meat white and dry looking, and although it is not harmful, the flavour and texture of the meat suffer. Freezer burn is avoided by careful packaging of the foodstuff before freezing. Removing air helps, and cooking quickly after purchase for foods especially susceptible.

In the fridge, salads can get soggy, as can some fruits. Storage, as we said earlier, in glass jars helps to slow this down, but still these foods are best eaten quickly. With salads particularly, it's best to prep and store the ingredients individually and combine just before eating.

Foods to keep on hand:

In addition to your weekly fresh food shopping spree, there are some ingredients that come up again and again, and are worth keeping stocked up in your cupboards.

Some can be replaced by fresh varieties, which are usually better, but a supply of dried versions is still worth having.

A well-stocked pantry means you won't fall short on ingredients.

Below are lists of ingredients to keep on hand—of course there are many other things you could add to this list, but it's a good place to start. These are all ingredients that have a long enough shelf life where you don't need to worry about them spoiling soon after you buy them, thus you don't have to have a specific plan for using them when you first buy them.

Ingredients For your Cupboard

Sea Salt/Black Pepper
Garlic and onion powder; ground spices
Tomato sauce, tomato paste, crushed tomatoes etc.
Fresh Garlic and fresh onions (these can keep for several weeks on the pantry shelf)
Canned vegetables
Powdered and liquid sweeteners
Almond flour
Coconut oil, coconut milk, desiccated coconut
Nuts and seeds
Olive Oil, Balsamic Vinegar, White Wine Vinegar

Vegetables:
A head of cauliflower (it features in so many dishes)
Two avocados
2 zucchinis
Four onions
Fresh garlic

In The Fridge
A carton of cherry tomatoes
1lb bag of baby carrots
A dozen eggs
A pound of butter
Cream
Yogurt

Remember to rotate the storage items around, especially the fresh ones. So, when you shop and buy a cauliflower, add it to storage and use the one that has been in the rack for the longest.

Chapter Summary

- Prepping meals can save a great deal of time
- Prepping helps you to stick to the diet you are seeking to follow
- Planning meals makes shopping easier, reduces waste and thereby saves money.

In the next section you will learn some recipes for each meal, starting with seven refreshing and awakening breakfast ideas.

Each recipe will be numbered in its section to make it easier for listing your weekly or bi-monthly menu, and will contain a list of ingredients, an explanation of how to make the meal, some tips on prepping, nutritional info and the number of servings in the recipe.

Breakfast Recipes

In this chapter you will learn some keto meal recipes that can be eaten for breakfast.

Number One - Sausage And Egg Muffin (Bread Free Sandwich)

This is a perfect starter breakfast. It is tasty and comforting, and will set you up for the day ahead. It is easy to prepare and will help you get into the swing of the keto diet.

Ingredients for the Dish
- Two Large Eggs (cook in egg moulds if you want a round shape)
- One tbsp. of butter
- One tbsp. mayonnaise (optional)
- Two sausages or sausage patties (cooked)
- Two slices cheddar cheese
- Slices of avocado

Prepping Advice
- Slice the avocado and cheese in advance. Wrap the cheese in film. Make the "egg muffins" ahead, and just microwave and top w/ avocado each morning.

Making the Dish
1. In a large pan, heat the butter at a medium temperature and put the moulds into the pan.

If you can't get pre-cooked patties, just fry them alongside your eggs.

2. Break the eggs into the moulds and gently mix with a fork. It takes about 3-4 minutes to cook the eggs, depending on the texture you like.
3. Remove the eggs. Take one, and add half the mayo, a cooked sausage patty, then half the cheese and the avocado.
4. Put the second sausage on top of the avocado, finish off with the cheese. Put the remaining mayo on the other egg, and complete the sandwich.

Nutrition Per Serving
Carbs 10.5 g
Calories 880
Fat 82g
Protein 32g

- Makes One Serving, multiply X number of days you want to eat this.
- Patties will keep in the fridge for up to four days.
- You can cook the eggs ahead if you want or the day of—it will only take a few minutes either way.

Number Two - Breakfast Loaf with Berry and Peanut Butter

A great option for those in a rush. The loaf can be made in advance. It will keep in a bread bin, wrapped in foil, for several days. It could be sliced and put in the freezer, then warmed in the toaster or oven.

Ingredients for the Dish
- ½ cup of peanut butter
- ¼ cup of butter, melted
- 5 eggs
- ½ cup of milk – coconut or almond milk can be substituted for those avoiding diary
- 1 tsp of vanilla extract
- ½ cup of flour – almond flour works especially well
- 3 tablespoons of sweetener
- 2 tsp of baking powder
- ½ teaspoon of sea salt
- ½ cup of mixed berries – frozen is fine

Prepping Advice
- Cook on the prepping day, or get the ingredients measured out at this point. This can make breakfast for 5 days for you, so it's great for weekday breakfast.

Making the Dish
1. Heat the oven to 350 degrees. Either use a silicon loaf pan, or use an ordinary loaf pan lined with grease-proof parchment paper.

A lovely alternative to bread.

2. Combine the peanut butter, melted butter and eggs in a large bowl. Mix until thoroughly combined.
3. Add the milk and vanilla extract, and mix.
4. Using a different bowl, mix together the flour, baking powder, sea salt and sweetener. Make sure that they are thoroughly combined.
5. Mix the contents of the first bowl into the second, stirring all the time.
6. Use a spatula to carefully fold the berries into the mixture.
7. Pour the contents into the loaf tin, and bake for approximately 45 minutes.
8. After 45 minutes use a toothpick or fine knife to check it is cooked, (the toothpick should come out clean). If necessary, cook for up to 15 more minutes, checking every five minutes.
9. Toast or eat fresh with butter.

Nutrition Per Serving (one slice) if using almond flour:
Net Carbs 5 g
Calories 150
Fat 15g
Protein 6g
- Makes approximates 5-6 servings.

This not only makes a great breakfast, but can also be used as a mid-morning snack, or as a light lunch.

Number Three - Keto Cereal

Cereal for breakfast is a great option. Quick to make, easy to prep, refreshing and full of long lasting energy. Keto diets and nuts go together brilliantly, and so do nuts and cereals. You can make up the ingredients well in advance, toasting several batches of nuts at one time and then simply store in the fridge.

Ingredients for the Dish
- 1-1/2 cup of unsweetened, shredded coconut
- Sweetener (to taste, optional)
- Small dash of salt (optional)
- ¼-1/2 tsp. cinnamon (to taste)
- 1 cup of toasted walnut pieces
- 1 cup of toasted macadamia pieces
- 1 cup of toasted flax seeds
- Milk

- Hint: to break nuts wrap in a tea towel and gently hit with a rolling pin until broken into smaller pieces – not too small or you lose the texture.
- Hint: toast nuts under a grill for one minute, or in a frying pan (shaking regularly to prevent burning, for one to two minutes. Or place on a baking tray in a medium oven for two to four minutes, checking regularly. The nuts should not burn, or a bitter taste will develop.

Choose your own selection of nuts if you want to personalise the dish.

Prepping Advice
- Make up a big bowl on your prepping day.
- Measure out a serving and add milk. Heat if preferred.
- This recipe makes 3 servings, but if you're making a big batch to store or freeze, just multiply x number of desired servings. (ex. Multiply ingredient amounts by 5 to get 15 servings)

Making the Dish
1. Simply combine the ingredients.
2. If desired, the contents can be heated gently. Serve with almond milk if desired.

Nutritional Information
Carbs 2 g
Calories 350
Fat 24g
Protein 22g
- Makes 3 portions.

Number Four - Ham and Cheese Waffles

Use plenty of melted butter to keep the waffles lovely and moist.

You can't beat a waffle, especially as a breakfast treat. However, this recipe works just as well as a light lunch or dinner.

Ingredients for the Dish
- 2 oz. of chopped ham steak
- 2 oz. of grated cheddar cheese
- Dried Basil and paprika to taste
- 1 tsp of baking powder
- 8 eggs
- A couple of scoops of protein powder (optional, can use can use almond flour)
- 12 tbsp. melted butter (tip – the butter helps to keep the waffles nice and moist. Don't skimp on it!)
- 1 tsp of salt (optional)

Prepping Advice
- Make the waffles in advance, reheating as required.
- Measure out the toppings in advance

Making the Dish

1. Separate 4 of the eggs into two bowls (separate yolk from whites) set the other 4 eggs aside.
2. Add the powder, baking powder, butter and sea salt to the yolks and whisk together.
3. Fold in the cheese and ham.
4. Whisk the egg whites together with the salt either with hand beaters or in the mixer until stiff.
5. Gently fold half of the whites into the egg yolk mixture. Leave for a few moments, then fold in the remaining egg white.
6. Add around a quarter of a cup of the mixture to a waffle maker, per waffle to be cooked. Cook for about four minutes until lightly browned.
7. Store in the fridge or freeze.
8. Heat the waffles in the toaster and while they're toasting, fry an egg on the stove top.
9. Serve an egg on the waffle, and top with paprika and basil.

Nutritional Information

Carbs 1 g

Calories 620

Fat 50g

Protein 45g

- Makes two portions.

Number Five - Baked Eggs...With Avocado

Sumptuous, oozing egg and smooth avocado, an unbeatable combination. A perfect breakfast for the whole family. Low carb and even more filling than a couple of slices of toast, this is also a quick and simple dish to prep, and can cook while you get on with morning chores, knowing that there is a treat awaiting in a few minutes.

Lovely egg filled avocadoes.

Ingredients for the Dish
- 2 medium avocado, cut in half with stone removed and skin left on.
- 4 medium eggs
- A pinch of garlic powder
- A pinch of sea salt
- A pinch of black pepper
- A small handful of grated Parmesan cheese

Prepping Advice
- Prepare the avocados and wrap in film if using within a couple of days.

Making the Dish

1. Preheat the oven to 350 degrees.
2. Cut the avocado in half, remove the stone and scoop out about a quarter of the flesh from each half. This is to create enough space for the egg.
3. Put the avocado halves in something to keep them stable, like a muffin tin.
4. Sprinkle the two halves with the sea salt, the black pepper and the garlic powder.
5. Crack the eggs so that one fits into each half. Sprinkle with the cheese.
6. Bake for about 12 to 15 minutes, or until the whites are set and are firm if the pan is shaken.

Nutritional Information

Carbs 3 g

Calories 261

Fat 20g

Protein 14g

- 4 servings.

Number Six - Cheese, Egg and Bacon Cups

A hearty breakfast which can be eaten hot or cold. You can cook up a load, and keep them in the fridge for the better part of a week, and simply reheat if you want to eat them hot. As with many other of the breakfast recipes, this lovely dish can be a light lunch or evening meal as well.

Ingredients for the Dish
- 6 strips of bacon
- 6 large eggs
- A large handful of spinach (frozen is fine if you can't get fresh)
- ¼ cup of cheese (a strong flavour works best, but go to your own tastes)
- Salt and pepper to taste

Spinach is a healthy and full flavoured vegetable of which we could make more use in our diet.

Prepping Advice
- Cook up in advance and reheat.
- Store in a plastic freezer or bag, or else layered on a plate wrapped in foil or plastic wrap with waxed paper between each layer.

Making the Dish
1. Preheat the oven to 400 degrees.
2. Fry up the bacon, and set aside to cool and drain. This could be prepped in advance.
3. Grease a muffin tin with oil, and line with a slice of bacon. Press the bacon down so the ends will stick up, these will become the handles with which you remove the cups later.
4. Beat the eggs in a bowl.
5. Drain and pat dry the spinach in some paper towels. Chop roughly (this can be prepped in advance) and add to the eggs.
6. Put about a quarter of the cup of the mixture into each muffin place, so that they fill it up to the three-quarter mark.
7. Sprinkle with cheese, and season to taste
8. Bake in the middle of the oven for about 15 minutes.
9. You can even freeze these and microwave for breakfast if desired.

Nutritional Information
Carbs 1 gram
Calories 101
Fat 7g
Protein 8g
- Makes six portions.

Number Seven - Yoghurt Parfait

This breakfast is totally prepare-able in advance, and in the morning simply add the layers as you fancy. You can prep your fruit and it will keep in the fridge for a few days – squeezing lemon juice onto it helps it to stay fresh. You can always tell with fruit if it is getting past its best as it will start to go mushy.

Refreshing and healthy, plus as tasty as can be. A perfect breakfast.

Ingredients for the Dish
- 2 c. tablespoons of natural, full fat yoghurt
- 1 cup of unsweetened, shredded coconut
- Sweetener (to taste, optional) – maple syrup works well.
- 1 cup of toasted walnut pieces
- 1 cup of toasted macadamia pieces
- 1 cup of toasted flax seeds
- 4 bananas, sliced (this adds sweetness, and could replace the sweetener listed above, depending on the sweetness of your tooth).
- 4 Handfuls of strawberries (sliced)
- 4 Handfuls of blueberries (sliced)

Prepping Advice
- This is best made on the day, but the ingredients can be prepared in advance, so it just needs to be put together.
- Note – choose the nuts that you like, and only toast if you like the flavour. This really is a recipe you can adapt to your personal likes.

Making the Dish
1. Take a glass serving jar, such as a Sundae dish or mug.
2. Place three tbsp. of the yoghurt in the bottom of the container.
3. Add sweetener if desired.
4. Add a layer of nuts.
5. Add a layer of the coconut.
6. Add the banana.
7. Alternate layers of fruit and nuts.
8. Pour the remaining yoghurt on top.

You can keep this in the fridge for a couple of days, although it is better to put the ingredients together just prior to eating, as the fruits will run into the yoghurt, and the nuts will lose their crispness if kept in the fridge ready mixed.

Nutritional Information
Carbs 9g
Calories 230
Fat 15g
Protein 20g
- Makes 4 servings

Notes:

- Experiment with the recipes, trying different ingredients and amounts to model the recipes to your tastes.
- These recipes are intentionally simple. Very few people want to spend a long time making breakfast (particularly on weekdays). Breakfast should be simple (one less thing to worry about in the morning.

Lunches

In this chapter we will give you some recipes for lunches that you can prep in advance, and then take with you to work or eat at home.

As with other recipes, these will be low carb recipes, with a high enough fat content to stave off pangs of hunger. They will include a wide variety of healthy food stuffs to help you both lose weight and maintain optimum health and energy.

Number One – Buffalo Chicken Lettuce Wraps

All kinds of fillings can be healthily wrapped in lettuce.

Fresh tasting and easily transportable, everything for this recipe can be prepared in advance and put with the lettuce on the day. The food will keep in the fridge three days at least.

Ingredients for the Dish
- ½ red pepper (diced)
- ½ green pepper (diced)
- 4 stalks of celery (diced)
- 2 lbs. of chicken thighs, skinless and boned, then chopped into bite sized pieced
- 2 scallions (sliced)
- ½ cup of crumbled blue cheese
- 2 tsp of onion powder, or a finely diced onion
- 1 tsp of garlic powder, or a crushed clove of garlic
- 2 tbsp. of butter
- Salt and pepper to taste
- Hot sauce to taste
- 8 large lettuce leaves

Prepping Advice
- Cook up and store, adding to the lettuce on the day.
- If you're packing your lunch for work, just put the buffalo chicken mixture in a container in your lunch box and include the washed lettuce leaves wrapped in plastic separately.

Making the Dish
1. Melt the butter in a large pan.
2. Add the peppers and celery and sauté for about five minutes
3. Add the chick, onion and garlic. Stir and season. Cook for about five minutes until the chicken is cooked.
4. Add the hot sauce (if using), stir and heat for another minute.
5. Remove the pan from the heat, and add the cheese and scallions, stirring all the time.
6. Put two or three tablespoons of the mixture into a lettuce leaf and enjoy.

Nutritional Information
Carbs 3 g
Calories 547
Fat 37g
Protein 50g
- Makes four servings of two leaf wraps per serving.

Number Two – Vegetarian Cauliflower Curry

Curried cauliflower, the light and tasty way to enjoy Indian cuisine.

This will keep until the end of the week if you prep on Sunday, and just goes to prove that great flavour can be achieved without meat and heavy carbs.

It is also a good one to fit in if you have had a few days of meat eating, to give the body a break. The keto diet is sometimes considered a little meat heavy, and this dish offers a tasty alternative.

Ingredients for the Dish
For the Main Dish:
- 1 head of cauliflower
- 1 ½ cups of full fat yoghurt (Greek)
- 2 tbsp. of curry powder
- 1 tsp of paprika (smoked)
- 1 tsp of pepper (cayenne for a kick)
- The juice of one lime
- 1 tsp of salt
- ½ tsp of black pepper
- 2 tsp of the zest of a lime

For the Topping:
- ¼ cup of drained, sun dried tomatoes
- ½ cup of pine nuts
- 1 tbsp. of cilantro
- 2 tbsp. of feta cheese, crumbled into small chunks
- ¼ cup of olive oil
- A clove of garlic

Prepping Advice
- Cook in advance and reheat

Making the Dish
1. Warm the oven to 375 degrees, and take a baking sheet lines with grease proof paper, or parchment paper.
2. In a large bowl, take all the main ingredients (not those for the topping) except the cauliflower. Mix them together then rub it all over the outside of the cauliflower head.
3. Cook for 45 minutes until the cauliflower is crispy and a lovely golden colour. Let it cool.
4. Make the topping. Put the garlic, sun dried tomatoes and half of the pine nuts into a blender and blast until chunky.
5. Add the rest of the ingredients for the topping and mix carefully.
6. Carefully cut the heads from the main cauliflower and place in shallow dish.
7. Drizzle the topping over the cauliflower and warm gently.

Nutritional Information
Carbs 7g
Calories 260
Fat 20g
Protein 10g
- Makes six servings. Stick the spare ones into the freezer.

Number Three – Beef Burritos

Tasty, storable, easily prepped ingredients and filling, a burrito makes a real treat for the middle of the week, when you need a lift to get you through the weekend. Beef is also one of the safest meats to store.

Something that adds to the ease of this dish is that the filling is made in the slow cooker, which adds to ease and convenience.

A lovely and tasty option, but remember to get low carb tacos.

This recipe makes four servings, and freezes well.

Ingredients for the Dish
For the Beef:
- 2 lbs. of sirloin steak
- 1 cup of chicken soup or broth (canned works well)
- 1 cup of BBQ sauce
- ½ of an onion, chopped up roughly
- 2 tsp of salt
- ½ tsp of black pepper
- 5 fresh cloves of garlic, crushed
- 1/2 tsp of cinnamon
- 2 bay leaves

For the Taco
- 8 low carb wraps
- ½ cup of mayo
- 1 ½ cups of coleslaw (you can make your own, but ready brought works just as well)

Prepping Advice
- Prepare the filling in advance
- Add to the tacos on the day.

Making the Dish
1. Pat dry the sirloin with paper towels, and score along the sides.
2. Combine the salt, pepper and cinnamon. Sprinkle it evenly onto the steak, making sure that there is an even covering.
3. Put the onion and garlic in the slow cooker. Place the beef on top and cover with the soup. Add the bay leaves and cook for eight hours.
4. When cooked, remove and strain the ingredients. Then shred the beef mix by pulling it with two forks.
5. Add the BBQ sauce and combine everything well.
6. Put some of the beef into the wrap, add coleslaw and dash of mayo. Wrap and eat.

Nutritional Information
Carbs 14g
Calories 750
Fat 50g
Protein 60g
- Serves four.

Number Four – Open-Faced Prosciutto and Brie Sandwich with Avocado Bun

We have a couple of sandwiches now. There are a couple of advantages with a sandwich. Firstly, it is easy to prepare. Simply prep the ingredients and put them together when you are ready to eat, or pack your lunch. Secondly, they are very easily transportable, so make an excellent addition to a picnic or work lunch.

This first is a sandwich with a difference – there is a notably absent ingredient.

Lovely, creamy brie – excellent with mushrooms and avocado

Ingredients for the Dish

- 1 avocado
- 4 small slices of brie
- 8 thin slices of prosciutto
- 6 mushrooms (any variety, but large flat ones work well)
- 2 cup of raw spinach
- 2 tsp of butter
- A pinch of sesame seeds
- Pinch salt
- A sprinkle of black pepper

Prepping Advice

- Measure out the ingredients in advance
- Cook up on the day you will be eating the sandwich

Making the Dish

1. Cook the spinach for five minutes until it has wilted. Drain and squeeze out excess water.
2. Slice the mushroom and sauté in the butter until soft. Add some pepper and salt.
3. Cut the avocado in half. Do this by cutting until the pit is reached, then rotating and twisting until the avocado splits. Remove the stone and scoop out the flesh. Cut a slice off the bottom of one half of the avocado so it can stand. This will be your 'bottom slice of bread'.
4. Fill the two halves of your avocado with the ingredients. Serve as open-faced sandwich

Nutritional Information

Carbs 12g
Calories 482
Fat 40g
Protein 16g.

- Serves 2

Number Five – The Keto Cubano

Warm for the weekend or holidays, cold for lunch at the desk, this meaty sandwich is built on low carb bread to keep it healthy and in line with the best Keto practice.

A Cubano is a sandwich containing pork loin, ham, pickles and Swiss cheese.

Ingredients for the Dish

- Thinly sliced dill pickles or ready-made pickle of your choice
- 1/3 lb. of thinly sliced cooked ham
- 1/3 lb. of cooked pork tenderloin
- ¼ pound of sliced Swiss cheese
- 1 tbsp. of melted butter or coconut oil to put on the paninis.
- 2 tbsp. of mayonnaise
- 2 tbsp. Dijon mustard
- Low Carb wraps OR bib lettuce

Make sure that you use low carb panini for this dish.

Prepping Advice
- Measure out the ingredients in advance
- Cook on the day

Making the Dish
1. Mix the mayo and mustard together and spread over the wrap (if using low carb wrap)
2. Divide up the pickle, cheese and meats between the sandwiches. Roll up the wraps tightly
3. Place in a sandwich maker, or in a panini press and cook for five to seven minutes.
4. If using the lettuce instead of the wraps, simply omit step 3.

Nutritional Information
Carbs 7g
Calories 472
Fat 36g
Protein 28g
- Makes four servings

Number Six – Keto Monkey Bread

Bread without the bread. This is a dish for which the ingredients can be readily prepared in advance, and it makes a fine breakfast as well as a lunch.

The eggplant, or aubergine, is the secret to keeping this bread low carb.

Ingredients for the Dish
- 2 baby eggplants, cubed
- ¾ cup of mozzarella cheese, shredded
- 2 tbsp. of melted butter
- 1 tbsp. of fresh basil, chopped roughly into small pieces
- 1 clove of garlic, crushed

Prepping Advice
- Cook in advance and reheat.

Making the Dish
1. Heat the oven to 375 degrees.
2. Take a muffin pan and lightly grease.
3. Combine the garlic, melted butter and a half of the basil.

4. Place some of the eggplant (four or five pieces) into the bottom of each muffin tray.
5. Sprinkle even amounts of mozzarella and drizzle butter mixture over each portion of eggplant
6. Add the remaining cheese on top and bake for around twenty minutes. The cheese should be nicely browned.
7. Allow to cool for five minutes and eat warm; you can reheat later.

Nutritional Information
Carbs 6g
Calories 195
Fat 15g
Protein 8g.
- Serves three.

Number Seven – Cauliflower Grists With Roasted Mushrooms And Walnuts

Just reading that recipe name makes my mouth water. All the ingredients can be measured out during the prepping session, and put together easily on the day. The savoury, cheesy taste is comforting and warming, and the dish is easy to prepare. The key is to get the cauliflower cooked right.

Ingredients for the Dish
- 6 mushrooms, sliced
- 3 cloves of garlic crushed
- ½ cup of walnuts
- ½ cup of water
- 1 cup of half cream, half milk (half-and-half)
- 1 cup of grated cheddar, as strong as you like
- 2 tbsp. of butter
- 600g (approx.) of cauliflower
- 2 tbsp. of olive oil
- 1 tbsp. of fresh rosemary
- 1 tbsp. of smoked paprika
- Pinch of salt (optional)

Prepping Advice
- To keep the grits nice and fresh, cook on the day.
- The ingredients can be measured in advance and prepped in advance.
- You can slice the mushrooms, grate the cheese, chop the cauliflower (in food processor), and just store in glass containers in the fridge

Making the Dish
1. Heat the oven to 400 degrees and line a baking tray with foil.

2. Combine the garlic, rosemary, walnuts, paprika and mushrooms with a touch of salt, and drizzle with oil.
3. Roast on the tray for fifteen minutes.
4. Cut and pulse the cauliflower heads in a processor until very fine, like rice.
5. Steam the cauliflower in a medium pot with a half cup of water. Do this for about five minutes as you want it tender, but not soft.
6. Pour in the half-and-half and simmer for three minutes.
7. Add the cheese and butter, and stir on a low heat. If the resulting mixture is not runny enough for your taste, add another half cup of water.
8. Add the hot mushroom and walnut mix to the top of the grits and eat warm.

The versatility of the humble cauliflower; a key to keto success.

Nutritional Information
Carbs 11g
Calories 452,
Fat 36g
Protein 16g
- Serves Four.

Number Eight – Spicy Roast Beef Cups

Another easy to make, easy to prep meal which is tasty, warming and filling. It makes a perfect lunch or a light dinner.

Ingredients for the Dish

Get the deli staff to slice your meat as thinly as possible.

- 6 thin slices of deli counter cooked roast beef
- 1 tbsp. of sour cream
- 1 ½ tbsp. of hot chilis
- ½ cup of grated cheddar cheese

Prepping Advice
- Cook in advance and reheat in your mug

Making the Dish
1. Break the beef up into small chunks, and layer half in the bottom of your cup, dish or mug.
2. Cover the beef with the cream sour, spreading it out.
3. Add a third of the chili
4. Spread a third of the cheese
5. Repeat numbers one to four.

6. Top with the remaining cheese and chili.
7. Microwave for a couple of minutes to melt the cheese.

Nutritional Information
Carbs 4g
Calories 270
Fat 18g
Protein 23g
- Serves one.

Number Nine – Crispy Pork Salad

The crispy crunch of pork belly, the fresh taste of salad, pear and bleu cheese (a match made in heaven) candied walnuts to add sweetness and texture and all finished with a light vinaigrette dressing. Summer perfection, and everything can be prepped in advance.

Yummy crispy pork belly.

Ingredients for the Dish
- ½ lb. of pork belly slices
- 1/3 cup of blue cheese
- ¼ of a pear, sliced
- 2 cups of salad leaves of your choice (rocket goes well with pear…)
- 2 tsp of salt
- 1/3 cup of chopped walnuts
- 1 tbsp. of stevia
- 1 tsp of water
- ½ tsp of Dijon mustard
- ½ tsp of any whole grain mustard for the dressing
- 2 tbsp. of white wine vinegar
- 2 tsp of olive oil

Prepping Advice

- Prepare all ingredients in advance, and store in glass containers. If packing your lunch, the morning of, assemble your salad, in a container and put the dressing in a separate container.
- Measure out the ingredients in advance.
- Do any chopping; a squeeze of lemon juice will help the pear chunks to stay crisp.

Making the Dish

1. Cover the pork with half of the olive oil. Cook in a hot oven until crunchy and browned, about 20 to 30 minutes.
2. Warm a pan and add the water and stevia to the pan, and add the walnuts once the stevia has dissolved. Cook for five minutes until the liquid has caramelised the walnuts.
3. Tip the nuts onto a tray and leave to cool. Note: they will be hot.
4. Chop the pear and cheese into bite-sized pieces.
5. Make the vinaigrette by adding the mustards, vinegar and oil into a bowl and mixing well.
6. By this time the pork should be cooked. Remove set aside to cool, then chop into bite sized chunks.
7. Toss the salad in the vinaigrette and add the pork, nuts, cheese and pear.

Nutritional Information

Carbs 5g
Calories 1050
Fat 55g
Protein 13g.

- Serves two.

Number Ten – Goat Cheese and Vegetable Salad

The trick with this is to char the vegetables to give them that caramelized taste. This is also a recipe that goes well without a dressing. It is a warm salad, and that means it works all year round.

Goats' cheese, a great mixer with salads, especially coated in our mixture below.

Ingredients for the Dish
- (4) ½-inch thick rounds of goat cheese
- 1 red or orange pepper, cut into eighths and seeds removed
- 4 cups of water cress
- 1 tbsp. oil, such as olive or avocado
- 1 quarter cup of sliced button mushrooms
- 1 tsp finely chopped onion
- 1 tsp finely chopped garlic
- 4 tbsp. of crunchy seeds – choose the ones you like, or mix and match. Sesame seeds are particularly good

Prepping Advice
- Measure out the portions.
- Cook the vegetables in advance.
- Cook the goat's cheese on the day

Making the Dish

1. Combine the seeds, onion and garlic in a dish.
2. Coat each piece of goat cheese in the mix, lightly coating both sides. Refrigerate.
3. Char the peppers and mushrooms in a pan with a spray of oil. Don't overcook, heat until the pepper starts to soften and darken.
4. Put the watercress into two bowls and add the pepper and mushroom to the top.
5. Fry the goat cheese on both sides, for about thirty seconds on each side. Take care flipping, as the cheese will already be starting to melt.
6. Add to the bowls, and drizzle with the oil.

Nutritional Information

Carbs 7g
Calories 350
Fat 28g
Protein 16g.

- Serves Two.

Chapter Summary

- Ten super lunches in this section should offer the incentive to pack your lunches for work.
- As with the breakfast recipes, use these as starting points for your own inventive lunches.

In the next chapter we will look at some dinner recipes.

Dinners

In this chapter you will learn twenty recipes for excellent, low cab dinners. Try them, and enjoy.

Number One – Pumpkin Soup

A warming pumpkin soup provides a comforting meal to end the day, filling you up in a relaxing way, turning the evening into a cosy experience.

Ingredients for this Dish
- 3 lbs. of pumpkin
- ¼ cup of olive oil
- 1 onion, chopped
- 2 tbsp. of unsalted butter
- 2 cups of coconut cream
- 1 tsp of salt
- 1 clove of crushed garlic
- 1 cup of water
- ¼ cup of pumpkin seeds

Prepping Advice
- Cook the soup at prepping time, and reheat as required

Making the Dish
1. Preheat the oven to 400 degrees.
2. Remove the seeds and pulp of the pumpkin. Chop into two-inch cubes.
3. Put the pumpkin on a baking tray, drizzle with olive oil and a pinch of salt. Cook for about 40 minutes.
4. While the pumpkin is cooking, cook the chopped onion in the butter for about eight minutes, until soft but not burned.
5. Blend the cream until it is light and whipped.
6. Add the onion, garlic and the rest of the salt to the cream mixture and blend.

7. Once the pumpkin has cooled, remove the skin and add the flesh to the other ingredients. Blend until completely smooth.

8. Warm in a pan, adding the water to thin the soup to taste. Sprinkle on the seeds once transferred to bowls.

Nutritional Information

Carbs 18g

Calories 500

Fat 30g

Protein 6g

- Serves six. Portions will keep in the fridge for three or four days, or can be frozen.

Number Two – Super Green Soup

This soup is full of superfoods.

Either prep by preparing ingredients in advance, or make in bulk and freeze what you won't be using that week.

Ingredients for the Dish
- 1 medium cauliflower head chopped into small florets
- 1 onion, chopped
- 2 cloves of garlic, minced
- 1 crumbled bay leaf
- 1 cup of watercress
- 2 cups of spinach
- 1 litre of vegetable stock (made from a cube is fine)
- 1 cup of coconut milk
- ¼ cup of coconut oil
- Salt and pepper to taste

The fresh greenness of watercress and spinach.

Prepping Advice

- Cook the meal at prepping time, and reheat as required

Making the Dish

1. Grease a pan with the oil and add the onion and garlic. Cook until slightly browned.
2. Add the chopped cauliflower and bay leaf, and cook for five minutes, stirring frequently.
3. Add the watercress and spinach and cook for three or four minutes until wilted.
4. Pour in the vegetable stock and bring to the boil, then cook for about 8 minutes until the cauliflower has softened a little, but still retains its firmness.
5. Add the coconut milk, take off the heat and blend until smooth and creamy.
6. The soup will keep refrigerated for five days, or can be frozen.

Nutritional Information

Carbs 7g
Calories 392
Fat 38g
Protein 5g

- Serves five to six.

Number Three – Cheese and Broccoli Soup

This is a particularly easy dish, great for beginners or those pushed for time. The whole family will love the cheesy taste.

Ingredients for this Dish

Lovely broccoli soup, with a cheesy twist.

- 1 cup of broccoli
- 1 cup of grated cheddar cheese
- 2 tbsp. of butter
- ½ teaspoon of xantham gum (a keto friendly thickener, but a tbsp. of almond flour will also work, although it will need to be sprinkled on through a sieve and stirred well)
- ¼ cup of onion
- ¼ cup of celery

- 1 ½ cups of chicken broth
- ½ cup of heavy cream
- Salt and pepper to taste

Prepping Advice
- Cook the meal at prepping time, and reheat as required

Making this Dish
1. Roughly chop the broccoli.
2. Put the butter, celery, salt and pepper into a pan with the better, and cook until the onions and celery go transparent.
3. Add the broccoli and cook for another three minutes, or until the broccoli has brightened its green colour.
4. Add the broth and cream, and bring to the boil.
5. Turn the heat down to simmer, adding the cheese slowly.
6. If you want to thicken the soup, add the gum or flour, and stir continuously until the soup thickens and any lumps disappear.

Nutritional Information
Carbs 5g
Calories 415
Fat 37g
Protein 14g.
- Serves three.

Number Four – Beef Stew

An easy, slow cooker recipe where there is almost no preparation but a brilliant, rich flavour at the end. If you don't like a spicy kick to your dinner, just take out the chili mix, it won't alter the texture. Or, add some sour cream or natural yoghurt when you serve.

Is anything as warming as a bowl of beef stew?

However, it is not a blow your brains out spicy meal. But it is one you will really enjoy.

Ingredients for this Dish

- 1 ½ lbs. of stewing beef cut into cubes (or, if you are really pushing the boat out, go for a better cut, such as sirloin)
- 2 cans of chopped tomatoes
- 1 tbsp. of chili mix – a ready-made shop bought one is fine
- 1 cup of beef broth
- 2 tsp of a hot chili sauce (optional)
- 1 tbsp. of Worcestershire sauce
- Salt to taste

Prepping Advice

- Cook the meal at prepping time, and reheat as required

Making the Dish

1. Turn the slow cooker on to low (or follow instructions on device).
2. Put in all the ingredients in and give a mix.
3. Cook for eight hours
4. Add salt to taste

Nutritional Information

Carbs 9g

Calories 222

Fat 7g,

Protein 27g.

- Serves six. Freeze spare portions or keep in the fridge for up to three days.

Number Five – Zesty Tacos with Keto Cheddar "Tortillas"

A great, really filling recipe with lots of cheese to fill you up. Serve with a little side salad, or if you want a keto friendly finger food for a buffet, cut the finished articles into bite sized medallions and serve.

A flexible, tasty and simple meal. And really, really, low in carbs.

Taco meat – make your own using the recipe below.

Ingredients in the Dish
For the Crust
- 2 cups of cheddar cheese

For the Topping
- 1 cup of taco meat, left over or following the recipe below
- ¼ cup of tomatoes chopped
- ½ an avocado, also chopped
- 2 tsp of taco sauce

- Any other toppings you like, such as diced onions, olives and so on

For the Taco Meat (to make a large amount)

- 1 lb. of ground or minced beef
- 1 tbsp. of chili powder
- A clove of garlic, crushed
- ¼ of a small onion, diced very small
- ¼ tsp oregano
- ½ tsp paprika
- Salt and pepper to taste
- Method – fry the beef for around 10-15 minutes, until cooked; add the other ingredients and mix well.

Prepping Advice

- Cook the meat at prepping time, and reheat as required
- Prep the toppings and add when required.

Making the Dish

1. Preheat the oven to 400 degrees.
2. Cover a baking tray with lightly buttered grease proof paper or baking parchment, leaving some 'handles' to make it easy to lift.
3. Sprinkle the cheddar to make a single layer completely covering the tray. Grate more cheese if needed.
4. Cook for about 15 minutes until the cheese bubbles and browns.
5. While the cheese is cooking, combine the remaining ingredients. Remember that the layers will need to be not too chunky as you will be rolling the taco later.
6. Remove the cheese from the tray, using the parchment 'handles'.
7. Add the ingredients to the cheese mixture. Keep it to a single layer.

8. Slice the dish using a pizza cutter or sharp knife from top to bottom, wide enough to hold its shape. Roll carefully from top to bottom.

Nutritional Information
Carbs 2g
Calories 491
Fat 35g
Protein 35g.
- Serves three.

Number Six – Veggie Bliss

The joys of fries without the bloating, or the calories.. Chop the vegetables during your prepping day and seal carefully, and they will still be crisp and firm after five days. If you feel the need for some additional protein, serve it with a couple of eggs.

Vegetable strips make an attractive alternative to potato fries/

Ingredients for the Dish
- 1 tbsp. of olive oil
- 1 head of cauliflower, using the florets – chopped – only
- ½ an onion, sliced into thin strips
- ¼ each of the following peppers, again all sliced into thin strips – green, red, orange
- Pinch of dill
- Salt and pepper to taste
- 2 large eggs, if wished

Prepping Advice
- Measure out and prepare the ingredients
- Cook fresh for the best results

Making this Dish

1. Heat the oil in a skillet or pan.
2. Put half an inch of water and add the cauliflower. Microwave for four minutes.
3. Fry the pepper and onions for a couple of minutes, then add two tbsp. of water.
4. Keep adding, a tbsp. at a time, water to the peppers and onion as they cook.
5. Add seasoning to the vegetables and mix.
6. Add the cauliflower and cook for another ten minutes.
7. If chosen, cook and add the eggs.
8. Hint: you could buy a ready-made fajita mix, and take out the pre-sliced onions and peppers.

Nutritional Information

Carbs 3g
Calories 145
Fat 12g
Protein 12g

- Serves One.

Number Seven - Bacon Burgers

These tasty and filling treats can be used as a meal in themselves, perhaps with a touch of salad, or as nibbles as part of a buffet. Easy to make, lovely cheesy and salty to eat they are a reminder that following a diet does not mean that fun goes out of the window.

Ingredients for this Dish
- 12 slices of bacon
- (12) 1-inch cubes of smoked cheddar cheese
- 12 sausage patties, raw
- Cumin powder to taste
- Onion powder to taste
- Salt and pepper to taste

Prepping Advice
- Prep the ingredients in advance
- Cook fresh for the best results.

Making the Dish

Ready for cooking.

1. Preheat the oven to a temperature of 350 degrees.
2. Get a baking tray and line with parchment or grease proof paper.
3. Put your sausage patties onto the tray.
4. Dust the sausages with the cumin, onion and salt and pepper to your taste.
5. Place a piece of cheese in the middle of each of the round sausage patties.
6. Make the sausages into a ball surrounding the cheese.
7. Wrap the bacon around the balls so that they are completely enclosed.
8. Bake for an hour. Then enjoy with your favourite dipping sauces.

Nutritional Information
Carbs 1 to 1.5g
Calories 250
Fat 20g
Protein 14g
  • Serves twelve (although you might find yourself eating more than one!)

Number Eight--Italian Meatballs

Wonderful Italian food is something that those on a Keto diet might miss out on. With heavy use of carbs in traditional dishes – pasta, dough and so on, it is a type of food that often does not fit well with Keto food. However, we can't miss out on our Italian, can we? So here is a dish that we can eat while on the diet.

The great taste of Italy, without any pasta.

Ingredients for the Dish
- 1 lb. of ground or minced beef
- 1 large can of whole, peeled tomatoes
- ½ cup of mozzarella, grated into slices
- 1 tsp of dried oregano
- 1 tsp of dried thyme
- ½ cup of red onion, diced into small pieces
- 2 cloves of crushed garlic
- 1 tbsp. of tomato paste
- Salt and pepper to taste
- A handful of fresh basil, roughly chopped, to garnish

Prepping Advice
- Cook the meal at prepping time, and reheat as required

Making the Dish
1. Preheat the oven to 375 degrees.
2. Mix together the herbs and ground beef and season with a touch of salt and pepper.
3. Form the mixture into sixteen meatballs.
4. Fry the meatballs for about five minutes, until they are browned all over.
5. Take out one tbsp. of the cooking juices from the pan, then add the tinned tomatoes, onion, tomato paste and garlic to the pan. Chop or break the tomatoes into smaller chunks. Simmer for ten minutes.
6. Put the meatballs in a dish and top with the tomato sauce.
7. Break the cheese into small chunks and spread over the tomato sauce
8. Cover the dish with foil, and bake for twenty minutes. Then, remove the foil and bake for five more to brown the cheese.
9. Throw on the basil and serve with a fresh green leaf salad for best results.

Nutritional Information
Carbs 8g
Calories 380
Fat 23g
Protein 25g

Bacon Leak Hush Puppies over Cauli-Mash

Ingredients for the Dish

For the Mashed Cauliflower (potato substitute)

- ½ a cauliflower or a full small cauliflower, cut into florets
- 2 tbsp. of whipping cream
- 1 tbsp. of butter
- Salt and pepper to taste

Cauliflower replaces the potato in this dish.

For the Hush Puppies

(Remember, substitute any of the veg below as desired)

- 3 slices of bacon, diced into small pieces
- 1 tbsp. of butter
- ¼ of an onion, chopped into small pieces
- 1 leek, sliced into rounds
- 1 green pepper, cut into chunks
- A couple of spring, or green, onions, cut into small pieces
- 1 cup brussels sprouts, chopped
- ¼ cup of Parmesan cheese
- ¼ cup of mozzarella
- 2 tbsp. of duck fat (substitute with olive oil or butter if you wish)
- 1 clove of crushed garlic

Prepping Advice
- Prep the ingredients by measuring out the items
- This can be cooked in advance, but is best freshly cooked.

Making the Dish

For the Cauliflower Mash
1. Put the cream, butter and cauliflower into a bowl and microwave on high for four minutes.
2. Mix well.
3. Microwave for another four minutes.
4. Blend until creamy.
5. Add the mozzarella while the mash is still hot, so that it melts into the mix. Set aside to cool.

For the Hush Puppies
1. Put a pan onto medium heat, and add the bacon, cooking until it is crisp, and any fat is gone. Take off the heat and put on a paper towel to dry out.
2. Add the tablespoon of butter to the pan, and cook the garlic for about one minute.
3. Add the onion and fry for another four minutes, but cut this short if the onion starts to burn.
4. Add the leeks and sprouts, and cook until soft, about seven minutes.
5. Add the spring onions and cook for just one minute
6. Take off the heat, but add the bacon immediately. Put with the cauliflower.
7. In another pan, heat the oil or duck fat. Shape the mixture into patties and dip roughly in the Parmesan.
8. Sear for a 2-3 minutes over a hot heat to form a crispy outside.

Nutritional Information

Carbs 9g
Calories 332
Fat 28g
Protein 10g
- Serves three.

Number Ten – Beef Welly (an update on the classic Beef Wellington)

Not for the faint hearted, this one. Beef Wellington is thought to be one of the hardest meat dishes to perfect, but get it right and it makes a spectacular dinner dish, ideal if you are entertaining, or want to treat yourself.

The traditional Wellington includes pate and a pastry coat, our version is more aligned to Keto expectations.

Ingredients for the Dish
- 2 tenderloin steaks (hint: don't skimp on the beef. Go for best quality, it will pay dividends.)
- 1 tbsp. of butter
- 4 tbsp. of liver pate
- 1 cup of mozzarella cheese
- ½ cup of almond flour
- Salt and Pepper to taste

Prepping Advice
- Measure out the ingredients
- This can be reheated, but for such a special dish, it is best cooked fresh

Making the Dish
1. Season the steaks to taste
2. Melt the butter in a pan so that it is sizzling but not burning. Put the steaks in the pan.
3. Sear all sides then take the steaks off the heat and allow them to cool.
4. Heat the mozzarella in the microwave for about a minute.
5. Stir in the almond flour while the cheese is still hot. It will form a dough.
6. Place the dough, while still as warm as possible, between two pieces of grease proof paper and roll flat.
7. Place a tablespoon of pate, about the size that the meat will cover, onto the dough. Spread it out so that it will encircle the meat.
8. Cut the dough so it will form a complete ball around the meat, when added, and the pate.
9. Put a piece of meat inside the dough, cut it and wrap it around the meat and pate.
10. Repeat for the other piece of meat.
11. Bake at 400 degrees for about twenty minutes, until the dough is a golden brown.

Nutritional Information
Carbs 2.5g
Calories 307
Fat 22g
Protein 26g
- Serves two

Number Eleven – Avocado Egg Pockets

A light and tasty dinner for when you don't have a lot of time, or are after a less heavy meal. A hint of a kick from the topping, and lots of protein and vitamins from the eggs and veggies.

Ingredients for the Dish
- 1 cup of diced zucchini
- 1 cup of chopped cauliflower
- 3 large eggs
- ½ a red pepper, chopped into small chunks
- 1 tbsp. of coconut oil
- ½ an avocado
- 1 tsp of smoked paprika
- ¼ of a finely diced onion
- A small, crushed, clove of garlic
- ¼ cup of grated cheese – something like a cheddar
- 3 tbsp. of cotija cheese
- 2 tsp of Tajin seasoning (a Mexican foodstuff)
- An optional tbsp. of jalapenos, sliced up

Prepping Advice
- Measure out the ingredients
- Cook fresh

Making the Dish

An all-time favourite – baked eggs.

1. Heat the oven to 400 degrees and line a baking tray with foil. Spread the zucchini, cauliflower and red pepper in an even layer.
2. Add the onion and garlic, then dust it all with the paprika.
3. Bake for 12 minutes.
4. Remove from the heat and add the cheese.
5. Slice the avocado and arrange around the vegetables.
6. Crack the eggs and bake for about ten minutes, until they are cooked the way you like them.
7. Add the cotija cheese, Tajin and jalapenos.

Nutritional Information

Carbs 6g
Calories 250
Fat 18g
Protein 6g

- Serves three.

Number Twelve – Chorizo Shakshuka

Another egg dish, but this time with a North African flair.

Tasty and filling, with a hint of the mysterious continent.

Normally, this is a vegetarian dish, and the chorizo can be replaced with extra peppers if you wish to have a meat free version.

Ingredients for this Dish
- 1 lb. of minced chorizo
- ½ cup of diced onion
- 1 large red pepper, diced into small chunks
- 1 tbsp. of coconut oil
- 3 or 4 crushed garlic cloves
- 1 large can of chopped tomatoes
- ½ tbsp. of chili powder
- ½ tbsp. of ground cumin
- 6 large eggs
- 1/3 cup of queso fresco, crumbled
- ¼ cup of cilantro, chopped up roughly
- Salt and Pepper

Prepping Advice
- As with most egg dishes, this is best baked fresh
- Measure out the ingredients at prepping time, and store in containers.

Making this Dish
1. Melt the coconut oil in a large heavy pan. Cook the chorizo for about eight minutes. Then remove the meat.
2. Add the onion and pepper to the now empty pan and sauté for about five minutes.
3. Add the spices and garlic and, stirring continuously, cook for another 90 seconds.
4. Add the tomatoes and return the meat to the heat. Simmer for fifteen minutes. If the dish completely dries out add a small amount of water. We want a little sauce, but not very much.
5. Using the back of a spoon, make six little wells and crack an egg into each.
6. Cook covered for between six (soft yolk) and ten (hard yolk) minutes, depending on how you like your eggs.
7. Take the lid off and crumble the queso fresco and chopped cilantro on top.

Nutritional Information
Carbs 7g
Calories 504
Fat 39g
Protein 30g
- Serves Six. The eggs will not store well, so reduce the portion size of the ingredients for smaller servings.

Number Thirteen – Salmon Fishcakes

A clever take on the traditional fish cake, making the dish even more flavoursome than usual. Serve with green saladnfor a light but very satisfying dinner. The fattiness of the fish works especially well in the keto diet. They will store in the fridge for a up to two days, or can be frozen.

Ingredients for this Dish
- 2 large eggs
- 4 ounces of sliced smoked salmon
- ½ tbsp. of butter
- 2 tbsp. of fresh chives
- Salt and Pepper
- Jar of ready-made Hollandaise sauce

Prepping Advice
- Cook the meal at prepping time, and reheat as required

Making this Dish
1. Boil the eggs for ten to twelve minutes. They need to be hard boiled.
2. Dice the salmon finely while the eggs are cooking.
3. Heat the butter under a high heat. Put half the salmon in to crisp it up, then set aside.
4. Run the eggs under cold water and peel.
5. Mash the eggs using a fork until they are broken up into fine pieces.
6. Take the raw salmon and half of the chives and mix with the egg and two to three tbsp. of Hollandaise sauce.
7. Split the mixture into four lumps and form into rough balls.
8. Mix the crispy salmon and remaining chives together and dip the egg balls into them until fully coated.

Nutritional Information

Carbs 1g

Calories 295

Fat 23g

Protein 18g

- Serves two.

Number Fourteen – Babyback Ribs

Here's a summer special, although if the weather's good enough for a BBQ it will work at any point of the year. Tender ribs that fall off the bone slathered in homemade BBQ will taste like summer no matter what time of the year it is.

Summer is here, the ribs are out.

Ingredients for this Dish

For the Ribs

- A rack of baby back ribs
- 1 cup of water
- ¼ cup of apple cider vinegar
- 2 tsp of liquid smoke
- 1 tbsp. of paprika
- ½ tbsp. of crushed garlic
- ½ tbsp. of diced onion
- ½ tsp of black pepper
- ½ tbsp. of chili powder
- ½ tbsp. of cumin
- ½ tsp of cayenne pepper
- ½ tsp of mustard powder
- 1 tsp of salt

For the BBQ sauce

- 1 ½ cups of mayo
- ¼ cup of apple cider vinegar
- 1 tbsp. of Dijon mustard
- 1 tsp of black pepper
- 1 tsp of salt
- 1 tsp of crushed garlic
- 2 tbsp. of your choice of sweetener
- 2 tsp of ready-made horseradish sauce

Prepping Advice

- Cook the meal at prepping time, and reheat as required
- Add the sauce only when ready to eat.

Making the Dish

1. Put the paprika, the half tablespoon of crushed garlic, onion, half a tsp of black pepper, the chilli powder, cumin, cayenne pepper, mustard powder and a tsp of salt in a bowl and combine.
2. Rinse the ribs in water and pat dry.
3. Remove the skin from the back of the ribs. To do this, place the tip of a sharp knife under the end of the skin and work the skin free, then pull carefully and it should all come away.
4. Rub the spice into the meat making sure it is fully covered.
5. Add the ribs, quarter cup of apple cider vinegar, water and liquid smoke to the put.
6. Seal the pot and cook on high for 35 minutes, allowing the steam to naturally release.
7. Meanwhile, whisk together all the remaining ingredients to make the sauce. Store the sauce in the fridge for at least two hours to allow the sauce to develop its flavour.

8. Preheat the grill to 450 degrees, and grill the ribs for about six minutes on each side.
9. Serve with the sauce.

Nutritional Information

Carbs 3g

Calories 650

Fat 42g

Protein 57g

- Serves five.

Number Fifteen –Garlic Cream Pork Chops

These will keep in the fridge, once cooked, for a couple of days, and all of the ingredients can be prepped in advance. The cream sauce keeps the chops moist.

Chops with a bit of a kick.

Ingredients for this Dish

- 4 boneless pork chops
- 1 tbsp. of paprika
- 1 tsp of crushed garlic
- ¾ of a chopped onion
- 1 tsp of black pepper
- 1 tsp of salt
- ¼ tsp of cayenne pepper
- 2 tbsp. of coconut oil
- 1 cup of sliced mushrooms
- 1 tbsp. of butter
- ½ cup of heavy cream
- 1 tbsp. of fresh parsley, roughly chopped

Prepping Advice
- Cook the meal at prepping time, and reheat as required
- Stir gently while reheating
- Best reheated at a low heat on the hob to stop the pork from drying out.

Making this dish
1. Mix together the paprika, garlic, one third of the onion you have prepared, salt, pepper and cayenne pepper. Sprinkle onto both sides of the chops and rub in.
2. Heat the coconut oil and brown the chops, about three minutes per side.
3. Take the chops and leave to one side.
4. In the pan, add the rest of the onions and the mushroom and cook for three or four minutes, until the onions go clear.
5. In a separate pan whisk the cream and butter under a low heat.
6. Put the chops and cream sauce back in the pan and cook for about five minutes in each side, making sure that the cream is stirred regularly.

Nutritional Information
Carbs 4g
Calories 481
Fat 32g
Protein 15g
- Serves Four.

Number Sixteen – Spaghetti Carbonara

OK, the spaghetti bit is a stretch of the truth, but who needs real pasta? This recipe includes shirataki noodles, which are usually to be found near the tofu and Quorn sections in the food aisle. But spiralized cucumber noodles, or zucchini will suffice if you prefer or cannot get the noodles.

Make sure you follow the carbonara part of the recipe precisely; experimentation is usually to be encouraged, but not with this creamy sauce, at least not until you are regularly making it.

Ingredients for this Dish

- 1 ½ tbsp. of butter
- 5 ounces of chopped thick cut bacon
- 3 packets of shirataki noodles, drained and rinsed OR you can use Spaghetti Squash if desired

Shirataki noodles are a must for anybody serious about a Keto diet.

- 3 large eggs
- 1 cup of grated cheese – Parmesan is best but go for a milder taste if you prefer
- 2 large minced cloves and garlic

Prepping Advice
- Cook the meal at prepping time, and reheat as required
- Get the tofu noodles packed in water that are ready to eat

Making the Dish
1. Melt the butter in a large, deep pan.
2. Cook the bacon until crispy.
3. Add the garlic, then the noodles.
4. Stir the noodles, as they heat.
5. While the noodles are heating, in a different bowl, beat the eggs and three quarters of the cheese.
6. When the noodles are fully heated, pop them into another bowl.
7. Stir the egg and cheese mixture while the noodles are still warm. The sauce should thicken to a thick consistency, but not solidify.
8. Top with parsley and the rest of the cheese.

Nutritional Information
Carbs 4.5g
Calories 361
Fat 29g
Protein 16g
- Serves four.

Number Seventeen – Shrimp in Tuscan Cream Sauce

The wonderful freshness, taste and texture of shrimps in a cheesy, creamy sauce. Serve on a bed of leaves, or with any vegetable that takes your fancy. Fish does not keep that well, and so follow instructions on the packet, or from the grocer, regarding storage – it will depend on whether the fish has already been frozen.

Shrimps in cream, easy to make and filling to eat.

However, the ingredients can still be prepped, then freshly put together. It doesn't take long.

Ingredients for this Dish
- 1 lb. of raw shrimp – buy cleaned with the tails removed
- 1 tbsp. of buttr
- 1 cup of cubed cream cheese
- ½ cup of whole milk
- 2 cloves of garlic, crushed
- 1 tsp of dried basil
- 1 tsp of salt
- ½ cup of Parmesan, or a milder cheese if you prefer
- 5 whole sun-dried tomatoes, cut into thin strips
- ¼ cup of baby kale

Prepping Advice

- Measure out those ingredients that you can in advance

Making this Dish

1. Melt the butter in a large pan.
2. Add the shrimp and lower the temperature.
3. Cook the shrimp for thirty seconds, then turn them and cook until they are beginning to turn pink.
4. Add the cream cheese.
5. Pour milk into the pan and increase the heat. Stir until the cheese has melted and there are no lumps.
6. Add the garlic, salt and basil and continue stirring.
7. Throw in the cheese, and finish stirring once it has melted in. Leave the dish to simmer until the sauce shows signs of thickening.
8. Finally add the tomatoes and kale.
9. Serve straight away.

Nutritional Information

Carbs 6.5g
Calories 298
Fat 18g,
Protein 23g

- Serves four.

Number Eighteen – Nachos con Carne

Comfort Keto. As with all nacho led meals, add and subtract from the recipe as you wish. The version here has a strong kick to it, but simple reduce the spices to cool it down.

No corn nachos in this dish, cauliflower shows its versatility once more.

Ingredients for this Dish

- 8 ounces of thinly sliced steak
- 1 tbsp. of butter
- 1/3 cup of coconut oil, use melted
- 1 ½ lb. of cauliflower
- ½ cup of cheddar cheese
- A small handful of sliced jalapenos (reduce the amount to make it less hot)
- 1 tsp of chili powder
- ½ tsp of turmeric
- 1 tomato, chopped into quarters
- 1/3 cup of sour cream
- ½ an avocado

Prepping Advice
- Cook the meal at prepping time, and reheat as required
- Add the topping prior to eating

Making the Dish
1. Preheat the oven to 400 degrees.
2. Slice the top off the cauliflower so that it breaks into chips.
3. Mix together the coconut oil, chili powder and turmeric, then toss the cauliflower in it.
4. Spread the cauliflower on a sheet, season and roast for twenty minutes.
5. While the cauliflower is cooking, prepare the rest of the dish.
6. Preheat a heavy pan and add the butter. Add the steak. Flip to cook the other side. Depending on how thick the meat is, this should only take a couple of minutes per side, perhaps less.
7. When the cauliflower is done, place it on a flat skillet
8. Slice the steak into small, fork sized strips.
9. Put on top of the cauliflower
10. Add the cheese and jalapeno and bake for five or so minutes until the cheese has melted.
11. Serve with the avocado (sliced), tomatoes and sour cream

Nutritional Information
Carbs 6g
Calories 385
Fat 31g
Protein 18g
- Serves five.

Number Nineteen – Zoodles with Avocado Pesto

The convenience and taste of zucchini noodles mean that they must feature in a dish or two. Easily made with a spiraller, and easily stored in sealed bags, it is a staple of the Keto diet.

However, this recipe is even easier, the noodles can be made without spiraler, but use one if you have one.

Ingredients for the Dish
For the noodles
- 3 zucchinis
- ½ tsp of salt

For the pesto
- ½ an avocado (if not fully ripe, add half a cup of water when turning into pesto)
- 1 cup of fresh basil
- ¼ cup of walnuts
- 2 peeled cloves of garlic
- ½ a lemon
- ¼ cup of grated Parmesan cheese
- 1 tbsp. of olive oil
- Leaves of fresh basil
- Salt and pepper to taste

Prepping Advice
- Get everything ready in advance, except for sautéing the zucchini
- Make the pesto ahead and store in a glass jar

Making the Dish
1. Use a vegetable peeler to slice the zucchini as thinly as possible.
2. Toss the strips with salt.

3. Gather together the avocado, basil, garlic, cheese, lemon and walnuts.
4. Put them all into a processor and pulp into a smooth paste. Add water if it is a little thick.
5. Grease a pan with a tbsp. of olive oil and heat.
6. Sauté the zucchini for three or four minutes. They will begin to go soft.
7. Gently add the pesto to the zucchini and toss carefully.
8. Garnish with fresh basil and the grated cheese.

Nutritional Information

Carbs 11g

Calories 325

Fat 26g

Protein 11g

- Serves two.

Number Twenty – Oven Roasted Sea Bass

A keto meal in disguise, and a perfect one for entertaining because the dish is easy but looks spectacular.

A highly decorous meal, which is much easier to bake than it looks.

Ingredients for the Dish
- 1 cleaned, descaled sea bass, otherwise whole (have the head removed if you prefer it that way)
- 1 cup of cauliflower, grated
- 1/3 cup of green olives
- 2 small lemons
- 1/3 cup of mint, chopped finely
- 1/3 cup of flat leaf parsley, chopped finely
- Salt and pepper to taste

Prepping Advice
- As a rather special dish, it is best cooked when ready to be eaten
- The individual items can be measured out in advance

Making the Dish

1. Preheat the oven to 400 degrees
2. Place baking parchment onto a tray and put the fish on top. Use one tbsp. of olive oil to rub into the flesh.
3. Season with salt and pepper.
4. Thinly slice one of the lemons and stuff the slices into the bass, along with a small amount of the herbs.
5. Bake for about 15 minutes.
6. While the fish is cooking, chop the olives into small pieces.
7. Juice the other lemon, and take the zest from the peel.
8. Mix together the cauliflower, remaining herbs, olives, lemon zest and juice along with two tbsp. of olive all, and season to taste with salt and pepper.
9. Serve the fish with the cauliflower salad.

Nutritional Information

Carbs 3.4g
Calories 380
Fat 26g
Protein 27g

- Serves two.

Chapter Summary

- We have provided some quick, some special and many tasty recipes
- The use of cauliflower and zucchini spirals can be employed in other dinners.

In the next chapter we will show you some easy to prepare freezer meals.

Freezer Meals

In this section we will cover meals that can be cooked and frozen, then defrosted and heated.

When defrosting, take them from the freezer in the evening and leave in the refrigerator overnight. The meals will then be ready to re heat the following evening. When reheating, the golden rule is that food needs to be piping hot throughout. That will ensure that any harmful bacteria that may have built up will be eliminated.

Here we have ten freezer meals suitable to be prepared and cooked in advance, then taken from the freezer when required. Cook as a part of your prepping time, and freeze.

Shepherds' Pie

The secret with this recipe is to really squeeze as much water from the cauliflower topping as possible. This is a recipe which lends itself particularly to freezing, as that process will help to dry the cauliflower even further. Also, the 'twice' cooked effect gained through reheating will add to the flavour of the beef

Ingredients
- 1 lb. of ground beef
- ¼ cup of chopped onion
- 3 cloves of garlic, crushed
- ½ cup of celery
- 1 cup of chopped tomatoes
- 1 head of cauliflower, riced or chopped finely, cooked and drained
- 2 cups of grated cheese
- ½ cup of sliced carrots

Making this Dish
1. Heat the oil in a large pan.
2. Brown the mince for a minute, then add the onion, garlic, celery, tomatoes and carrots.
3. Cook for another five minutes.
4. Put into a large oven dish, and top with the cooked cauliflower. Add the cheese to the top.
5. Heat the oven to 350 degrees and cook for 40 minutes.
6. Take out of the oven and cool as quickly as possible.
7. Either freeze in the dish, or divide into portions and freeze.
8. Take out of the freezer at least 12 hours before eating.
9. Take the lid off the container, and place a piece of paper towel on the cauliflower topping to soak up any excess water.

10. Reheat until piping hot throughout, you may wish to add a touch more cheese at this point.
11. The food will keep for three to six months easily.

Nutritional Information
Carbs 6g
Calories 469
Fat 39g
Protein 23g
   • Serves four.

Chicken Curry

This is a low carb version of a tasty Indian recipe, and freezes very well. Serve with riced cauliflower, or a steamed mixed vegetable medley

The taste of the mystery; a brilliant curry completely in tune with a Keto diet.

Ingredients for the Dish
- 2 lbs. of boneless and skinless chicken thighs
- 3 large tomatoes, chopped (tinned works as well as fresh)
- 1 cup of chicken stock
- 1 can of coconut milk – make sure that it is unsweetened
- 1 tbsp. of lime juice

For the spicy curry paste
- 1 chopped onion
- 2 finely diced cloves of garlic
- A small handful of toasted peanuts
- 3 small red chilis chopped into small pieces
- 1 tbsp. of fresh grated ginger, or half a tsp of ground ginger
- 1 tbsp. of water

- 2 tsp of coriander ground
- 1 tsp of ground turmeric
- 1 tsp of ground cinnamon
- 1 tsp of ground cumin
- 1 tsp of ground fennel seeds
- A large pinch of black pepper
- Parsley for decoration

Making the Dish
1. For the paste – place all the ingredients listed in this section and blend into a paste in a food processor.
2. Cube the chicken into bite sized pieces.
3. Using a wok if possible, or frying pan, heat the paste in olive oil for three or four minutes stirring continuously, then add the chicken and cook for two more minutes.
4. Add the tomatoes and chicken stock and stir in. Once the food is simmering, reduce the heat to stay at this level and cook for thirty minutes.
5. Add the coconut and cook for a further twenty minutes. Stir occasionally.
6. Add the lime, salt and pepper (to taste)
7. Take off the heat and cool quickly. Place into freezer pots and freeze. Reheat by microwaving until piping hot throughout. Add a dash of water when doing this to rehydrate the food. Decorate with parsley.
8. The dish will keep for three to six months in the freezer.

Nutritional Information
Carbs 7g
Calories 430
Fat 22g
Protein 53g
- Serves four.

Coconut Chicken Soup

This Thai dish is full of flavour, and is perfect for freezing. Simply heat on the stove until piping hot when you are ready to eat it.

Ingredients for the Dish
- 6 cups of chicken broth
- 2 stalks of lemongrass
- 1 lime
- 1 tsp of freshly grated ginger
- 1 lb. of boneless chicken thighs, or the equivalent weight of chicken breast. In either case, chopped to small pieces.
- 2 cups of chopped mushrooms
- 1 ½ cups of coconut cream

Making the Dish
1. Heat the broth in a pan.
2. Rough up the lemongrass to release its aroma, then cut into about one-inch pieces.
3. Add the lemon grass, ginger and salt to the pan.

4. Juice the lime, and add some of the zest, then put these into the mix.
5. Simmer the broth for twenty minutes then strain away any solids.
6. Add the chicken and mushrooms to the strained broth and cook for twenty minutes in the pan.
7. Remove the chicken and break into as small of pieces as possible.
8. Put them back in the broth, and add the cream.
9. Cook for another five minutes.
10. Cool and freeze.
11. The product will keep for nine months in the freezer.

Nutritional Information
Carbs 7g
Calories 325
Fat 20g
Protein 29g
- Serves four.

Zesty Lamb Meatballs

You can make a number of the meatballs and then simply take the ones you need, defrost and cook up with goat's cheese, cauliflower rice and mushrooms.

Super flexible and super tasty, lamb meatballs.

Ingredients for this Dish
- 1 lb. of ground lamb
- 1 large egg
- 1 tsp of fennel seed
- 1 tsp of salt
- 1 tsp of crushed garlic
- 1 tsp of pepper
- 1 tsp of paprika

Additional ingredients
- 2 tbsp. of coconut oil
- 1 onion, diced small

Making this Dish

1. In a large bowl combine all the ingredients except the additional ones.
2. Shape into a dozen meatballs then put aside.
3. Heat the coconut oil and onion in a pan for eight to ten minutes.
4. Add the garlic and heat for another couple of minutes
5. Add the meatballs and cook until there is no pink showing on any side. They should be firm to the touch.
6. Take off the heat, cool quickly and portion off. Put in the freezer until ready for a meal.
7. The food will keep for six months in the freezer.

Nutritional Information

Carbs 3.5g
Calories 495
Fat 41g
Protein 27g

- Serves four.

Herbed Chicken Thighs with Roasted Vegetables

When cooking up meals for the freezer, we will want some that are quick, simple and use little that will need to be washed up. At the same time, these meals need to be tasty. This straightforward dish of chicken thighs meets those needs.

Keeping the skin on chicken thighs helps to keep them moist and succulent when cooking.

Ingredients for the Dish
- 4 boneless chicken thighs, with the skin on
- 2 zucchinis
- ½ cup of sliced carrots
- 2 tbsp. of olive oil
- 2 tbsp. of balsamic vinegar
- (1) 1-inch cube of ginger, minced
- 1 tsp Italia Seasoning
- Salt and Pepper to taste

Making the Dish

1. Preheat the oven to 350 degrees.
2. Season chicken with salt pepper and Italian seasoning.
3. Arrange the thighs on a greased baking tray.
4. Slice all the vegetables and arrange them around the chicken.
5. Mix the oil, vinegar and ginger, and spread over the food.
6. Bake for thirty minutes.
7. Cool quickly, divide up into portions. Freeze.
8. Defrost and reheat in the microwave until piping hot. Serve with cauliflower mash.
9. This meal will keep for three to six months in the freezer.

Nutritional Information

Carbs 2g
Calories 375
Fat 32g
Protein 22g

- Serves four.

Lemon Shrimp with Roasted Asparagus

Tasty, tangy and refreshing, the fine sharpness of lemon and texture and meatiness of shrimp make a perfect combination and, as an added bonus, this is a simple dish to prepare.

Ingredients for this Dish
- 12 asparagus stalks, cut into two-inch sections
- 2 tablespoons of butter
- 1 ½ lbs. of shrimp
- 1 tsp of lemon pepper
- 1 tsp. lemon zest
- 1 clove of crushed garlic
- ½ tsp of salt
- 2 packets of shirataki noodles (optional)
- Lemon wedges (for serving)

Shrimps with lemon, fresh and zesty. Serve with shirataki noodles for a filling meal.

Making the Dish
1. In a large bowl, place the shrimp and add half of the butter. Sprinkle on the lemon pepper, lemon zest, add the garlic and toss with a little salt.
2. Add the shrimps to the tray, pushing the asparagus to one end.
3. Cook for another seven or eight minutes.
4. Cool and freeze.
5. When ready to serve, heat the shrimp in the sauce over the stove. Serve over cauliflower rice or tofu noodles
6. Make the Asparagus the day of: Preheat the oven to 400 degrees. Spread the asparagus in a layer on a tray and

drizzle with half of the melted butter. Add a dash of salt and pepper and toss the asparagus.

7. Bake for four minutes.

8. Depending on the type of tofu noodles you purchased, open the package, drain the water, and rinse. Serve the hot shrimp and sauce over the noodles w/ lemon wedges.

9. This meal will keep for three to six months in the freezer.

Nutritional Information

Carbs 5g

Calories 240

Fat 12g

Protein 25g

- Serves four.

Guacamole Salmon

Another simple but very tasty dish. Reheat in the microwave, with a few drops of water, to prevent the salmon from drying out.

Full of Omega 3 oils, salmon fillets are an extremely healthy food option.

Ingredients for this Dish

- Salt and Pepper
- ½ tsp garlic powder
- 1/2 tsp. dried dill
- 2 salmon fillets
- 1 avocado
- ½ a lime
- 2 tsp of diced red onion
- 1 tbsp. cilantro
- Cauliflower – for serving with the meal

Making the Dish

1. Season salmon with salt, pepper, garlic powder and dried dill.
2. Cook the salmon, skin down, for about five minutes in a lightly oiled pan. Then flip the salmon over and repeat on the other side.
3. Cool and freeze.
4. When ready to eat, defrost and reheat carefully in the microwave, checking every thirty seconds of so.
5. Rice the cauliflower and heat in a lightly greased pan for about eight minutes.
6. Blend together the avocado, the juice from the lime, the cilantro, and the onion until smooth.
7. Serve the salmon on the riced cauliflower, and add the avocado sauce on top.
8. This meal will keep for three to six months in the freezer.

Nutritional Information

Carbs 5g
Calories 420
Fat 27g
Protein 35g

- Serves two.

Roasted Garlic Soup

A full soup which is warming, tasty and perfect for a light dinner or a warming meal on a cold night.

Another extremely healthy dish, the benefits of garlic to human well-being is considerable.

Ingredients for this Dish
- 2 complete garlic bulbs
- 3 chopped shallots
- 1 large head of cauliflower chopped into small pieces
- 6 cups of broth
- ¾ tsp of salt
- Ground black pepper to taste.

Making this Dish
1. Preheat the oven to 400 degrees.
2. Peel the garlic bulbs but keep intact. Cut off a small amount of the top and place on a square of foil with some olive oil. Cook for thirty-five minutes.

3. Allow to cool, then squeeze out the garlic from each bulb.
4. Pour the rest of the oil in a pan, and cook the shallots for about six minutes. Do not let them burn.
5. Add the garlic and all the other ingredients to the pan, and simmer for twenty minutes.
6. Blend the soup until it is smooth.
7. Cool and freeze. Reheat in a saucepan when ready to consume.
8. This meal will keep for nine months in the freezer.

Nutritional Information

Carbs 9g

Calories 73

Fat 2.2g

Protein 2g

- Serves two to three.

Stuffed Peppers

These can be made in advance and reheated or frozen. It is a very flexible recipe, and you could add grilled bacon, or chorizo chorizo to the mash, but we have gone for ease and speed here.

Ingredients for the Dish
- 1 head of cauliflower, trimmed to small florets
- 4 red or yellow bell peppers, cut in half and deseeded.

The recipe here uses cauliflower to stuff the peppers, but any chopped up veg will work.

- 1 tbsp. of olive oil
- 2 cloves of crushed garlic
- 1 tbsp. of butter
- Pinch of black pepper
- 1 cup of grated cheese
- 1 lb ground beef, browned

Making the Dish

1. Steam the cauliflower for around eight to ten minutes until soft.
2. Brown the beef until fully cooked. Season with salt and pepper.
3. Meanwhile, heat the oven to 350 degrees.
4. Put the cauliflower in a blender with the butter, garlic and pepper.
5. Blend until smooth. Mix in the ground beef.
6. Lightly coat the pepper halves with the oil.
7. Spoon the cauliflower/beef mixture into the pepper halves. Top with a sprinkling of cheese (you can add this when reheating if you intend to store and reheat the peppers, which is best done in the oven over a low heat.
8. Cook for fifteen to twenty minutes, until the pepper begins to char and the mixture is hot.
9. Store and freeze.
10. To Serve, heat in preheated oven (300 degrees) on a cookie sheet, until hot and sprinkle with grated parmesan.

Nutritional Info:

Carbs: 12.5g

Calories: 260

Fat: 10g

Protein: 17g

- Makes 4 servings

Old Fashioned Beef Stew

Just because it is traditional, expect to be surprised by the freshness of the flavours of this great version of a classic recipe.

Is there anything as warm and homely as a bowl of beef stew?

Ingredients for the Dish

- 1 lb. of beef for stewing, chopped into bite sized pieces
- 2 cups of beef broth
- 4 cloves of crushed garlic
- 1 diced onion
- 1 chopped up yellow pepper
- 2 cups of chunky carrots
- 2 cups of chunky radish
- A pinch of salt and pepper
- ½ tsp. Corn starch (to thicken if necessary)
- 1 tbsp. of butter
- 1 tbsp. of coconut oil

Making the Dish

1. Heat a large pan and add the coconut oil. Brown the beef on all sides, then move aside.
2. Add the onions and garlic to the pan, plus the butter, and cook for two to three minutes. Scrape the bottom of the pan to keep those flavoursome pieces.
3. Add the broth and cornstarch
4. When the mixture comes to the boil, add the beef back in. Simmer for thirty minutes
5. Add the vegetables and cook for another thirty minutes. Add water if the stew begins to dry out.
6. Cool and freeze. Simply reheat on the hob when you want to eat it.
7. This will keep for six months in the freezer.

Nutritional Information

Carbs 5g

Calories 432

Fat 35g

Protein 19g

- Serves four.

Chapter Summary

- Use the storage chart in the opening chapter of the book to check for how long meals can be stored in the refrigerator.
- Many of the other meals in this book can also be cooked up and frozen. Check the section in part one which deals with foods not suitable for freezing if you are unsure.

In the final section we will look at some last minute, throw together meals….

Last-Minute Side Dish Ideas

In this chapter you will learn how to make some salad dressings which can be stored ready and be waiting for use. In addition, we have included some last minute, quick to throw together dishes for those rushed moments when you don't know what to serve with your main dish.

Because many of the dishes are thrown together as a last-minute dish, we have excluded the nutritional information since it will depend on portions and ingredients as to the actual figures. However, rest assured that all of these dishes are low carb.

Number One – Classic Oil and Vinegar Dressing

These two simple ingredients combine to make a perfect dressing.

This is the simplest of dressings, and is just sumptuous. Many readers will use it already, but for those who have not heard of it, it is so easy, keeps for ages and brings the taste out of any salad stuffs.

If you have a non-keto guest, it works as well on a baked potato or for dipping bread.

Ingredients for the dish
- 6 tbsp. of good quality extra virgin olive oil
- 3 tbsp. of good quality balsamic vinegar

Making the Dish

1. The easiest imaginable recipe – simple mix the two ingredients.

2. Note – the two will quickly separate, but just re stir with a small fork or mini whisk.

3. Change the ratio in the quantities to suit your own personal taste. I find that the 2:1 balance works best, allowing enough balsamic to come through when the dressing is poured but without the sweetness overwhelming the delicate oil.

4. If you're feeling fancy, squeeze in half a lemon and reduce the vinegar and sprinkle in 1 tsp. Italian seasoning.

Bacon and Mustard Dressing

Something a little different here, and it does take a little extra time to prepare, but the salty flavour is brilliant with a light, sweet salad.

Crispy bacon, not an ingredient you might associate with a dressing, but it adds a lovely salty twang.

Ingredients for this Dish
- 3 tbsp. of bacon fat
- 1 tbsp. of Dijon mustard
- 1 tbsp. of red wine vinegar
- 1 small shallot chopped up very finely
- Salt and pepper to taste

Making the Dish
1. Drain bacon grease from grilled bacon (you could then use the bacon in your salad)
2. Whisk together the mustard and vinegar.
3. Gently fry the shallots until softened
4. Add the shallots to the mixture, and stir in the bacon fat. Add salt and pepper to taste.
5. Serve immediately, while hot.
6. This will store in the refrigerator for three days, and can be reheated before serving.

Throw together salad

Now we have some ingredients for throw together salads. Chop these up and keep in the fridge, and simply add a dressing from the list above.

Ingredients for this Dish
To be honest, whatever takes your fancy, but the ingredients below make a nice combination of textures and flavours.
- Rocket leaves
- Diced Peppers – green, red, yellow – the variety of colours makes any salad look great

Coloured peppers make any salad burst with life and vibrancy.

- 2 radishes, roughly chopped – to give snap and a kick
- Baby tomatoes
- Sesame seeds
- A handful of cashews

Making the Dish
1. Take the salad vegetables out of their containers in the fridge, and mix together.
2. Add the nuts throughout.
3. Top with the seeds.
4. Simply drizzle with the dressing of your choice.

Zucchini Spirals

These brilliant noodles make a great alternative to cauliflower rice or mash. Simple to make, and will keep sealed in a zip up bag for four or five days in the refrigerator. You do need a spiraliser, but that is an investment that will pay for itself several times over, letting you make your own fresh vegetable noodles rather than buying pre-sliced versions, which are expensive and do not last as long.

A great addition to ANY meal, prepare in advance and store in a sealed, portioned bag in the fridge.

Ingredients for this dish
- 4 zucchinis
- 1 tbsp. of olive oil
- Salt and pepper
- 1 tbsp. butter
- 1 tbsp. Italian seasoning

Making this dish
1. Spiralise the zucchini. Separate into four fridge bags. Take them out when ready for eating.
2. Heat the oil in a pan, and add the noodles for three to four minutes. Or you can boil them in water

Cauliflower Puffs

These can be made and stored in the fridge for half a week. Or they can be frozen and added as a side dish to your dinner (they will even make a light meal in themselves with a little salad.)

Ingredients for this Dish

- 1 head of cauliflower, cut into florets
- 1/3 cup of sour cream
- 1 cup of grated cheese
- 3 cloves of crushed garlic
- 2 eggs
- 2 egg whites
- Salt and Pepper

Making the Dish

1. Preheat the oven to 400 degrees, and grease a muffin tray.
2. Put a steam basket into a saucepan, and fill the pan with an inch or two of water.
3. Add the cauliflower and garlic, and steam for ten minutes.
4. Transfer to a blender and puree to a smooth consistency.
5. Stir in the cream, cheese and salt and pepper. Add the eggs until they too are well blended.
6. Beat the egg whites until they form stiff peaks.
7. Add to the main mixture with a careful folding motion.
8. Spread between the muffin trays and bake for around 20 minutes.

After beating egg whites, fold them into the mix carefully, making sure that you do not exclude the air.

Egg Muffins

These are another side that can make a full meal, and can be made in advance and frozen.

A savoury and versatile meal.

Ingredients for the Dish
- 6 eggs
- 1 finely chopped scallion
- A cupful of cooked bacon, broken up
- ½ cup of grated cheese
- Salt and pepper to taste

Making the Dish
1. Preheat the oven to 350 degrees.
2. Whisk the eggs with the salt and pepper, then stir in the cheese.
3. Spread the batter through a lightly greased muffin tray, then add the bacon.
4. Cook for fifteen to twenty minutes, until golden brown.

Last Minute Grill with Asparagus and Pepper

Prep the ingredients at the weekend for a great quick meal when you know you will be rushed for time.

Ingredients for this Dish
- 8 stalks of asparagus

Asparagus – delicious in any form but especially grilled.

- 2 red peppers
- 1 clove of garlic, crushed
- Salt and Pepper
- 1 tbsp. of olive oil

Making this Dish
1. Chop the red peppers into thin slices.
2. Put the asparagus on a grill tray lined with foil.
3. Add the peppers.
4. Top with the oil, garlic, salt and pepper.
5. Grill under a high heat for five minutes, checking that the vegetables do not burn.

Chapter Summary

- A well-stocked cupboard and well prepped fridge will mean that it is easy to throw together last-minute recipes
- That's the joy of cooking for Keto, it is all about simplicity.

Final Words

There you have it! A book of amazing yet simple and tasty keto recipes.

Remember though, that this is a book about saving time. And the best way to do that is to prep your food on your self-appointed prepping day.

I hope that you can see that cooking or reheating is also a quick and straightforward job.

As you become more comfortable with your Keto diet, experiment with these dishes, adapting them to your personal tastes, and those of your household. Very few need to be followed to the letter to deliver excellent results.

And enjoy your Keto experience, feeling lighter, energized and with more time and money to enjoy.

There are so many wonderful dishes that fit with the low carb requirements of the Keto diet. Try making your own. This one is avocado stuffed with eggs and bacon. Try substituting the bacon with smoked salmon...or ham...or crispy pork...

About the Author:

Andrea Adams apart from being an author, is an entrepreneur, activist and proud wife and mother. After quitting her corporate job at a prestigious marketing firm in Denver 5 years ago, she started a health food café with her sister, Marta. The café was a great success and has since opened several other locations in Colorado. Andrea only works part-time in managing the business and has taken a step back to focus on her real passion: creating recipes and writing.

When she is not experimenting in the kitchen, you'll find her hiding in a quiet corner of the house plugging away on her laptop— that is, when she is not cheering in the stands at her sons' football games or helping them with their homework. She also fosters stray dogs and helped found a shelter for injured and abused animals. She now lives in Boulder with her husband and three sons.